THE FURNITURE OF HEAVEN

THE FURNITURE OF HEAVEN
& OTHER PARABLES FOR PILGRIMS

MIKE MASON

REGENT COLLEGE PUBLISHING
VANCOUVER

The Furniture of Heaven & Other Parables for Pilgrims
Copyright ©1989 by Mike Mason

First published 1989 by Harold Shaw Publishers, Wheaton, Illinois

This edition published 2002 by Regent College Publishing
an imprint of the Regent College Bookstore
5800 University Boulevard, Vancouver, B.C. V6T 2E4 Canada

Scripture references are a combination of the NIV (New International Version) and the author's own paraphrases. We gratefully acknowledge permission to use The Holy Bible, New International Version. Copyright © 1973, 1978, 1984 International Bible Society. Used by permission of Zondervan Bible Publishers.

We gratefully acknowledge *Soundings: A Journal of Poetry and Prose From the Regent Community* who first published "The Heart of the Mountain" in Spring 1988; *Union Life* for "Christopher Rainbow" in March/April 1988; *Rainbow Harvest* for "How the Chipmunk Stripes" in 1986.

All rights reserved. No part of this publication may be reproduced, stored in a retrieval system, or transmitted, in any form or by any means, electronic, mechanical, photocopying, recording of otherwise, without the prior written permission of the author, except in the case of brief quotations embodied in critical articles and reviews.

National Library of Canada Cataloguing in Publication Data

Mason, Mike, 1953–
The furniture of heaven, and other parables for pilgrims

ISBN 1-55361-055-5 (Canada)
ISBN 1-57383-102-6 (United States)

1. Parables. I. Title.
PS8576.A7956F8 2002   jC813'.54   C2002-910799-7
PR9199.3.M3928F8 2002

for Harry Robinson,

and for all the people
of St. John's Shaughnessy

*He whose walk is blameless
has ministered to me.*
Psalm 101:6

Contents

The Heart of the Mountain   1
The Chancellor of the Exchequer's
   Private Audience   13
The Furniture of Heaven   23
The Golden Meteor   37
The Great Author   57
Christopher Rainbow   75
Jessica and the Talking Tree   83
How the Chipmunk Got His Stripes   95
Scarecrow   109
What Really Happened at Multnomah Falls   125
The Garden of the Beatitudes   143
Stumbling Stone   149
George and the Dragon   159
Yes, Mr. Church, There Is a Jesus   169
The Anteroom of the Royal Palace   179
Dreambums   189
The Last Day   195
Tutankhamun   213
Pinocchio   219
And His Train Filled the Temple   227
The Time Machine   237
True North   257

Ah, Sovereign Lord!
They are saying of me,
"Isn't he just telling parables?"
Ezekiel 20:49

The Heart of the Mountain

IN THE DAYS when the West was young, two brothers, Seth and Theo, settled on a homestead in a remote and rugged valley at the foot of a towering mountain. After several seasons of backbreaking toil, it became clear to them that the land was not as choice as they had first hoped. While on the surface the soil appeared rich and black, rain fell but stingily in those parts, and the growing season turned out to be unexpectedly short. Year after year the brothers picked rocks, cleared brush, and wrestled with the elements, yet still their crops came up sparse and stunted.

Like almost any spot on earth, the valley could often appear spectacularly beautiful. But the longer the brothers lived there, the more the wild glory of the place seemed to mock them with its inhospitableness. Winters were bitterly cold and stormy, and in summer the sun was a blister in the painfully bright sky. The whole region was like a paradise that was right in front of the eyes, yet somehow could never be entered. In addition to all the other hardships endured by the settlers, the mountain that loomed above their heads assumed a kind of hovering *presence*, almost as though it were haunted, or as though constantly threatening to come down upon their heads.

In spite of all this, the two brothers were a hardworking, good-living pair, who somehow managed to eke out a meager living from the stubborn soil. As poor as poor could be, they yet were able to wrest from their labors enough satisfaction to carry them through each day and into the next. And what more, realistically, could men ask out of life than that?

One frosty morning in early fall, Seth and Theo were surprised to wake up and find a goat standing in their yard. Although from time to time these creatures could be glimpsed high up on the mountain slopes, they were not known to frequent the valley, and domesticated goats were unheard of in those parts. However, as the brothers approached the animal she gave the impression of being perfectly tame, and allowed them to stroke her, to lead her into a corral, and even to milk her distended udders. Moreover, upon sampling this milk, they found it to be rich, creamy, abundant, and sweet as honey—in short, a product far superior to the insipid trickle of stuff that issued from their one cow. Where, they wondered, could such a fine and well-fed animal have come from?

For several days the brothers enjoyed this welcome gift from their mysterious guest. But one night, abruptly, just as inexplicably as the animal had appeared, she disappeared. Seth and Theo awoke in the morning to an empty corral, and though they searched the valley from one end to the other, not a trace of the wayfaring goat was to be found.

"Why didn't you let me tie her up as I suggested?" complained the elder Seth to his younger brother, as the bitterness of their loss set in. But sharp words and hard feelings could not bring the treasure back.

Instead, some days later, it happened that the goat returned of her own accord, reappearing just at a point when the brothers had given up all hope of ever seeing her again. This time they tethered her securely in the barn, and now the ambrosial milk tasted even more delicious to them than it had before.

Following a brief stay, however, once again the goat broke loose, and again no amount of searching could locate her. And so it came to pass that a kind of pattern began to develop, a haphazard though somewhat predictable pattern, in which every few days the animal would turn up out of the blue in the brothers' farmyard, and then just as suddenly she would vanish. Wherever it was she went off to, always on her return she would be healthy, sleek-coated, and laden with milk, as though having grazed her fill of sweet grasses in some lush and verdant pastureland. And while it was certainly true that the brothers had little enough of their own with which to feed the goat, still they made every effort to keep her from straying, yet all without success. For the creature seemed possessed of an infinite capacity for outwitting them.

One evening Theo, the younger brother, came up with a novel suggestion: "Instead of attempting to keep the goat here," he proposed, "why don't we try following her when she leaves? After all, wherever it is she disappears to, the land there must be much richer than our own, and it cannot be very far away."

Yet how were the men to know when the goat was about to depart? "No problem," said Theo. "We'll fasten one end of a long cord to our friend's tail, and the other end I'll tie around my own wrist. That way, as soon as I feel a tug I'll know that she's ready to leave, and then we both drop whatever we're doing and follow her."

Although this seemed a simple enough plan, the actual implementation of it was not so easy. For it meant that during the next several days Theo had to accomplish all his chores around the farm with a long leash attached to his wrist. As awkward as this was at first, nevertheless he managed to complete his share of the work as usual, and was actually surprised at how accustomed he grew to the inconvenience.

Seth, however, found the situation an endless source of amusement, and was constantly making snide comments such as: "It's a good thing my kid brother is tethered, or I'd be afraid he might run away on me!" Or: "So tell me, little brother, who's tied to who?"

One dark night, in the wee hours, Theo felt a gentle tug on his cord. Rising quickly from bed and throwing on some clothes, he hurried into the next room and shook his elder brother by the shoulder.

"Come, my brother, it's time!" he urged, as the tugs on the rope grew more insistent. "Come, our goat is leaving! It's the moment we've been waiting for!"

But it so happened that Seth had had a hard time of it that day, and had gone to sleep exhausted. In the middle of the night, in a warm bed, it seemed a foolish thing indeed to get up and go chasing off after some fickle, wandering goat.

"Go back to bed, my brother," he murmured sleepily. "Let's wait for another opportunity. The goat will come back."

When Theo shook Seth more vigorously, the latter responded angrily. "Don't you know what time it is?" he snarled. "Besides, only one of us needs to go. If you insist on running after this old nag, why not do it by yourself? Then you can return and tell me the way." And with that, Seth rolled over and went back to sleep.

Theo could wait no longer. Already he was being drawn irresistibly out of the room and down the stairs into the yard. It was a still, cold, incredibly black night, so dark that he could see no trace of the goat ahead of him, nor even make out his own feet. It was the sort of night in which one seemed to remember things one had never known, and with nothing but the pull on his wrist to guide him (almost as though this were no mere animal, but a person leading him gently yet urgently by the hand), the young man walked with strange assurance past the enormous shadow of the barn, through the unseen gate of the corral, and out into the frost-hard laneway.

Then after a while he felt his feet treading uphill, along a stony path. Sure enough, the goat must have headed in the direction of the mountain. The path would go on for a mile or so, Theo knew, and then it would come to an abrupt halt at the base of some sheer cliffs. And what was to happen then?

Up and up and over boulders and fallen trees they climbed, always rising, until finally they stood right beneath the towering shadow of the cliffs, where for the first time Theo caught a fleeting glimpse of the ghostly, white-bearded goat up ahead. She seemed, in fact, to be directly above him, walking straight up the vertical rock face! And then, all at once, without quite knowing how, the young man found himself following in her steps. He felt his feet gripping one tiny toehold, then another, and then sidling along the narrowest of rock ledges—narrow, almost, as a wire, narrow as the very cord tied around his wrist. And so up he went, straight up the precipice, poised and canny beyond any ken, his body melting like a shadow into the solid rock wall.

But this was only the first in a series of bewildering and impossible obstacles which, so long as Theo gave way to the sure tug of the rope against his flesh, he somehow managed to navigate with wondrous ease. Eventually, toward dawn, he heard a great sound of rushing water ahead, and then once more he caught sight of the goat, disappearing now behind the silver curtain of a high mountain waterfall. Following his guide through the cascade, and getting thoroughly drenched in the process, he was led next down a long dark tunnel full of twists and turns which finally emerged quite suddenly into an enormous open expanse, a sort of great subterranean cavern but without any walls, and dazzlingly illuminated. And there, in astonishment, Theo stopped short and rubbed his eyes.

Intuitively, he understood that this new interior world he had entered into was somehow the very heart of the mountain itself, the hollowed-out bosom of the rock! No sun was to be seen here, and yet the earth underfoot and everything in sight seemed to pour forth radiance and warmth, as though light and energy were emanating from within things. Overhead stretched not a stone ceiling, but a firmament of watersmooth silk, appearing deeper and more limitless (if such were possible) than the sky itself. Even the skin on the man's own hands shone with a lustrous color for which there was no earthly name.

The landscape here, for all its strangeness, had much the appearance of an alpine meadow, lushly carpeted with luminous emerald grasses and spangled everywhere with tiny star-like flowers. Nearby flowed a river, clear as new wine, and along its banks silver-leafed willows dense as haystacks seemed literally to drip with honey. In the distance flocks and herds grazed over gently rolling hills, and there were fields of thick ripe grain and orchards heavy with all kinds of fruit. As far as the eye could see, here was a land rich and fat and beautiful, overflowing with bounty.

How surprised and delighted the young man was to discover such a luxuriant garden paradise existing so very close to his own desolate homestead—indeed, just the skin of a mountain away! Without further delay he untied the cord from his wrist, knelt down beside the goat, and throwing his arms about her neck he wept in joy and gratitude, praising her again and again for having led him so strongly and surely to this heavenly place.

Yet as full to the brim as his heart was just then, at the same time Theo could not help but feel a stab of remorse as he recalled his elder brother Seth, now left alone down below in the harsh barrenness of the valley. That very moment this lifetime partner of his would be going about the drudgery of their daily chores, almost certainly trying to accomplish the work of two, while entirely oblivious to the reality of this marvelous paradise so nearby.

At first Theo could think of nothing else but of returning to the valley at once to fetch his sibling. Long experience, however, had taught him that an elder brother does not listen to a younger brother when it comes to such things, and most probably would not even believe him. Besides, he knew that only the goat herself could guide a man along the tortuous path that led up the sheer rockface of the mountainside.

Accordingly, taking pen and paper from his pocket, Theo scribbled a brief note which read:

Dear Brother—
I am writing to you from a brand new land the glory of which is beyond description. Please believe me, this place is everything we have dreamed about, and it makes our little acreage look like a desert! You must join me here, and to do so you need only tether the goat to your hand, just as I did, and follow her up the mountain. Please come without delay.

Next Theo rolled up his note into a little tube and inserted it carefully into one of the goat's long ears.

Though at present she was grazing contentedly, he knew that shortly she would return once again to the valley and stand in the front yard of the brothers' homestead, tacitly proffering her milk. Then Seth would come out of the house and welcome her, patting her on the head, whereupon the animal would wiggle her ears and the note would fall out. Although the skeptical elder brother might take a little time to mull matters over, soon enough he would be convinced, or at least intrigued. One thing would follow from another, and before long the pair would be reunited.

Satisfied then that he had done everything within his power, Theo went off happily to explore his abundant new paradise, from which all that was lacking was the presence of the one person closest to him in the world. And sure enough, after a few days of grazing in the lush meadows the goat did return as predicted down the mountainside, following the laneway back to the homestead, and finally standing placidly in the front yard, just as she had done so many times before.

By this stage, however, Seth had begun to grow angry over Theo's long absence, with a simmering anger that gave way gradually to fear, and a gnawing fear that spawned a yet more burning anger. What business had that kid brother of his running off after a stray animal? And abandoning him to do all the work of the farm alone? Indeed, if the rash fellow weren't dead by now, at the very least he'd be lying in a pile of rocks somewhere with a broken leg, and would need to be rescued. And with a whole vast wilderness out there to comb through, how did the little fool ever expect to be found? Men were not made to go chasing after mountain goats!

Sullenly, smolderingly, out of the corner of an eye Seth stared and stared at the silent white creature standing quietly in the yard. Yet all day long he would not go near her, not even to collect her milk. For in his heart he thought: "That goat is nothing but a troublemaker. Sure, she gives good milk. But she's also the bearer of ill fortune. She has led my brother astray, and now she dearly wants to entice me too. She would be the death of us both! But I won't give in. I'll not fall into her trap."

When, therefore, the man finally did approach the goat, it was not to pat her lovingly on the head. No. Nor did the animal wiggle her long ears, as the younger brother had expected. And neither did the all-important note come tumbling out onto the ground. No.

Instead, what happened was that just as dusk was settling over the valley and the sky was turning a smokey red, suddenly all the elder brother's suppressed anger and fear came boiling out, and he was gripped with an overwhelming passion. And creeping up behind the goat, with one decisive stroke Seth split open her fine and gentle head with an axe.

And only then did his eyes fasten on the note, and only then did he recognize Theo's handwriting. But by the time he read the words, they were already soaked in blood.

* * *

Once the owner of the house gets up and closes the door, you will stand outside knocking and pleading—"Sir, open the door for us!" But he will answer, "I don't know who you are, or where you come from."
　Luke 13:25

The Chancellor of the Exchequer's Private Audience

YOU MUST UNDERSTAND—I've been moving in court circles for quite some time now. I mean, before being appointed Chancellor of the Exchequer, I'd held half a dozen different portfolios. You name it, I've done it. I wasn't born yesterday.

But let me tell you something: My private audience with the King the other day made quite an impression upon me. It's amazing how radically it changed my whole view of things, and particularly my view of *him*: the one on the throne. Before, of course, I'd seen him lots of times. But usually, I have to admit, it was from a distance. Even on the few occasions when I'd been close enough to talk to him (though naturally I hadn't dared), it was always in a room full of people—never alone.

And so, as incredible as it may sound, I'd never actually met the King for myself, face to face. Seems almost comical, in a way—me being the Chancellor of the Exchequer and all.

It's not as if there hadn't been chances. But I guess I'd never wanted to admit to myself that it was all that important, or significant to my career. I mean, around court circles there's always a lot of chin-wagging about the King. But the fact is, nobody really takes him that seriously.

In any case, through no planning of my own, suddenly I found that the moment was upon me. The time had come when it was just him and me, one on one. It sort of happened by accident, the way an elevator will stall between floors, and all at once you find yourself thrown into intimate contact with a stranger.

I guess the first thing that surprised me was how calm and unhurried he was. Here I'd always figured he was a busy person with not a moment to spare, just like myself. Yet now he gave the distinct impression of being cool as a cucumber and having all the time in the world.

Naturally I took the opportunity to yap my fool head off. In spite of the fact that inside I was feeling at a total loss for words, I had learned how to keep a conversation going. (Yet why was it, I wondered, that

The Chancellor of the Exchequer's Private Audience

I always seemed to end up talking too much—or else not at all—around people I wanted to impress?)

Not that I did any apple-polishing, mind you. Quite the contrary—I'm afraid I was really quite blunt with the King. In fact, you might say I spilled my guts to him.

Secretly, I guess, I'd been waiting a long time for this. Suddenly there seemed to be a lot at stake. So right off the bat I let him have it, between the eyes and with both barrels. All the stuff that was pent up inside me, all the complaints, all the personal and political criticism (not only of others but of himself), all the things I'd often imagined being able to say to him in just this sort of situation—it all came tumbling out.

I suppose he just struck me as the sort of person who might appreciate directness. But honestly—the things I heard coming out of my mouth! Even I was shocked by my boldness.

And the thing that amazed me, and had the effect of egging me on, was the way the King just sat and took it all. Sat and listened. And not the way most people do, keeping quiet and smiling innocuously, just to humor you. No—I knew without a doubt that the King was giving me his undivided attention. He was hearing and weighing everything.

I'd known he was a quiet man. But he didn't say a word to me. Not one word! I tell you, it gave me a jolt. It brought me up short. And the result was, I just ran out of steam. I got to the end of my wind, and had nothing more to say. Then something very odd happened: For the longest while, the two of us simply sat and looked at each other.

It was clearly his turn to talk. Any other person would have said *something*, anything at all, if only to be polite. Yet still he said nothing. He seemed to be listening. Listening to *me*—as if to my thoughts. And I felt in those few moments more sheer quietness than I ever had in all the rest of my life put together.

I tell you, it was uncanny. And the longer this went on, this sitting and listening, the more it seemed that his quietness began to enter into me, into my very thoughts. It was like drinking a magic potion, something rich and delicious and intoxicating.

It was almost like receiving a transfusion of blood. As though some great ocean were flowing deep and slow into my own puny veins. And somehow I got the message that, at that point, our meeting had just begun.

For up until then, I realized, I hadn't really been talking to the King at all, but only to an *image* of him. Not to the real person, you see, but to a figment of my own imagination.

You know how it is. I guess, in spite of myself, I'd spent so much time practicing for this moment— thinking what I would say, and what he would say, and then what I would say, and so on (making up fine speeches, you see, and delivering them to the inside of my own head), that when it came to meeting with

The Chancellor of the Exchequer's Private Audience

the real King face to face, I was right out of my depth. I had no idea how to handle it. To be honest, I might as well have been sitting at home and talking to myself, only pretending that the King was present.

And another thing was, I'd done so much talking *about* him. You know, one moment bragging what great friends we were, and the next moment grumbling and gossiping behind his back. Everybody does that. And I suppose, up to a point, it's all right. But I wonder why more people don't try speaking their opinions and complaints (to say nothing of their praise) directly to his face? For talking *to* a person, and talking *about* him—they're two entirely different things. Like night and day. Especially when it comes to the King. I found that out.

I guess the big mistake I'd always made was in thinking that the King must be just like everybody else—not quite *real*. Not *all there*. Always sort of off in his own little world, planning his own agenda.

Let's face it, people are like that. It's hard to get their attention. No matter how good they are, there's always something phony, cardboard, two-dimensional about them. Especially in court circles. But you get used to it. In most people, phoniness is something you just have to forgive, or at least excuse or ignore. After all, people are only human.

But when it's the King—when there's the least hint of inattentiveness, artificiality, or corruption in the *King*—then that's a different matter. That's something you can't forgive. Because if he's really the King—then let him be perfect! Let him bloody well see to it that he's spotless as a lamb! What I mean is: If he's no better than anybody else, what's he doing up there on the throne? Who's he kidding? That's what I've always said.

And that's what everybody I know has always said. Not that they'll talk that way out loud, necessarily. But the way people *act*, when it comes to the King—well, you'd think he was nothing but an old fool. Really. I did it myself for years. It's the classic situation of a monarch with no power. A nice figurehead, but no clout. That's how I always saw him.

But one thing I'd never done: I'd never gone to the King himself, to find out if it was so. To stand in his presence and get his side of the picture: that's the thing.

Truth is, I guess I was afraid. Afraid that maybe he did have power, and that maybe just to be around him—even for a moment or two—would be like dynamite or something. That he'd blow me up, or blow me away. Or that he'd change me, irrevocably, so that I'd never be the same again. Just because that's the sort of person he is.

And sure enough, that's exactly what happened. That one private consultation of mine with the King was a more earthshattering event than anything else I had ever experienced. It completely revolutionized my life.

The Chancellor of the Exchequer's Private Audience

In fact: *I never lived before I met him.*

Can you imagine what it was like for me to find out that everybody I'd ever listened to had been dead wrong about the most important person in the world? And that he—the very one whom all the rest of us so loved to blame, to dismiss, to ridicule, to murmur against—he was the one who was in the right? He, in fact, was the only one in the right. About everything.

I tell you, it sort of boggled the old mind. Especially looking around and seeing what a sad state things are in. Because I know what you're thinking: If it's true that the guy is so perfect and wonderful and all, then why doesn't he get busy and clean up the royal mess around here? If he's really got clout, why doesn't he up and use it? Pull out all the stops—right?

I used to think that way, too. But as I say, my one meeting with the King himself changed my thinking. Of course the place is in a mess. But the King—believe me—he knows what he's doing. And he's not just sitting on his fanny, either.

So as far as I'm concerned, the world can go ahead and grumble. Let the pundits make their gloomy pronouncements; let the Senators and the Supreme Court Judges vent their hot air; let all the Cabinet Ministers stand up on their tables and wave their fists, or run naked through the streets if they want to; let all the rabble go stark raving mad, and my own life collapse around me in ruins ...

But listen: If the King knows what he's doing, that's good enough for me. That's all I need to know.

I'd like to tell you a lot more about this, about my personal audience with the King. But I'm afraid there isn't a whole lot more to say. All we did, the two of us—I swear—was sit there and gaze into each other's eyes. For a long, long time. Just him and me.

No quick solutions to all the problems of the Kingdom; no instant answers or eloquent theories; no empty promises; no stop-gap measures. Nothing like that. In fact, no talk about politics at all.

But instead, for the first time, I was able to look in the eye of the guy on the throne, and see him as he really is—pure and sovereign, and uncluttered by all my prejudices. And I saw him like that, I think, simply because of his amazing graciousness in allowing me, in his presence, to be who I really am.

He didn't try to change me. So I went away changed.

And now, let me tell you, life is sure a whole lot different around the Treasury Department! Because now things are done the King's way. And now this stuffy old Chancellor of the Exchequer can hardly contain the gladness he feels over having seized that opportunity to meet personally with His Majesty. For the mysterious thing I discovered was this: that he's the only person you *can* meet with that way—face to face. Far from being unapproachable, he's the only one who *is* approachable. Eminently approachable.

The Chancellor of the Exchequer's Private Audience

Everybody else has got something to hide. But he's wide open as the sky.

You can waste a lot of time haggling and fooling around with politicians and courtiers. But if you go straight to the top, you'll discover that the King is the only one who will really hear you out, and level with you.

He's the only one who doesn't have an axe of his own to grind, an image to keep up, a face that needs saving.

I guess that's why he's the King.

When I tried to understand all this,
  It was oppressive to me—
Until I entered the sanctuary of God:
  Then I understood.
    Psalm 73:16-17

The Furniture of Heaven

IN THE VILLAGE of Aix-la-Croix, next door to the little parish church, there lived a cabinetmaker named Simon Cyr who dreamed of creating the finest furniture the world had ever seen. In fact, his dream was loftier even than that, for he wished by his art to transcend the world itself.

Simon Cyr's father, and his grandfather and his great-grandfather before him, had all been carpenters. But young Simon had no desire for carpentry. Although he loved wood, he did not want to spend his life pounding nails into it, swinging a hammer, framing buildings. No, his longing was to do something more delicate and beautiful with wood, something more amenable to perfection. He wanted to design furniture.

One of his earliest memories was of being with his father one day when a sudden thunderstorm came up. All morning as the boy had played in the workshop, a summer rain had been falling, drumming softly on the roof and bringing out the sweet smell of the sawdust and new wood. But around noon, as father and son sat in the open doorway eating their lunch, the clouds had blackened dramatically, and they heard the first rumblings of distant thunder boiling up throatily from the cauldron of the horizon.

"You hear that, Simon?" his father had said, taking the boy in his lap. "That means they're moving around furniture upstairs."

Before long the rain had turned to huge dark drops hurtling out of the bruised sky as though launched from catapults, and next door the little church looked like a ship being tossed on high seas. Forks of lightning flashed over the grain fields like great trees made out of light, and soon thunder was crashing directly overhead and then growling away across the sky like a thousand grand pianos rolling over a hardwood floor.

Furniture, thought the boy. *They're moving around furniture upstairs.*

Always after that, whenever there was a thunderstorm, this memory returned to him. Often his father would reinforce it, telling him again the meaning of the thunder. It was as if this were something very important for a boy to learn, yet at the same time something which even a father did not fully comprehend. Was there really another world up there beyond the clouds? A world with houses and furniture?

From the beginning Simon had dimly grasped, with a child's intuition, that this place "upstairs" must be equivalent to heaven. And like all children, he wondered what it might be like, this airy upper realm with its mysterious goings-on. Would he himself one day make furniture worthy of being placed in one of the rooms up there in heaven? Might he with his own hands create objects glorious enough to rouse the thunder?

Many times as he grew older he helped his father build staircases, and this became his favorite task in carpentry. He liked the feel of the way the treads and risers and stringers all fitted together like an intricate puzzle—especially where the steps had to bend round a corner. Every piece in a winding staircase was fine, exact, handmade, and being a perfectionist, Simon was pleased with such things. But when it came to installing the handrail he was often disappointed, for his father would be content with nothing better than a rough board or two, square and uncomfortable to the palm. All that seemed to matter was that it was secure. But didn't a fine staircase deserve a fine railing, thought the boy? Didn't one climb with the hands as well as the feet? And shouldn't there be provision for those who might like to slide on their way down?

"Simon, Simon!" his father would laugh. "We're not building a roller coaster—just a set of stairs!"

But Simon envisioned gleaming banisters, polished newels, and ornately turned balusters. As a little boy he had even dreamed of a colossal stairway that would reach right up through the clouds and into heaven, where the thunder was. As the years went by, he had different visions of it: sometimes a delicately winding helix, made of laminated rosewood and ebony, elaborately tooled; or other times a wide, wide flight of oakbeams, straight as a highway and broad enough for the whole world to ascend at once ...

As a teenager Simon Cyr designed and built his own workshop, alongside his father's, where in his spare time he began turning out chairs and tables, bookshelves, dressers, and cabinets. Soon he was selling these to the local villagers, and later in neighboring towns. Within a few years his name was known throughout the countryside, for he worked with the energy of vision, and the things he made were both beautiful and functional. Even when it became clear that not only was he supporting himself financially, but in fact was earning more money than his father, still he strived to keep his work simple and practical, and thereby to justify his artistic leanings.

"A true masterpiece," he liked to say, "should be something sturdy enough to bear the weight of a man. That is why architecture is the greatest of all the arts, and cabinetmaking is the most exquisite branch of architecture. Beautiful paintings hang on walls in museums, and good books sit on shelves waiting to be opened and absorbed. But furniture is used everywhere, everyday, by everyone. That is its great beauty."

As his reputation grew, Simon Cyr found he had more and more freedom to indulge his imagination. He began coming up with radical new designs for the commonest household articles. He built sculptured tables, circular desks, chairs from a single piece of wood. He created huge china cabinets that gave a breathtaking impression of weightlessness and grace. The reviews of his first gallery show described his work as "music in wood," and before long he was receiving important commissions. For the lobby of a new theater he designed panelling that incorporated every known variety of wood in the world. And for an academy of music, he built a central staircase with a balustrade in the form of a xylophone that could really be played!

Although Simon never lost sight of the goal of functionalism, his work grew progressively ornate. He was fond of lamination, intaglio, and hand-carving. And because he made increasingly lavish use of scrolls and curlicues and fretwork patterns, these early years of his career came to be known as his baroque phase. He loved working with the most colorful woods—knotty pine, bird's-eye maple, the swirl-grained oaks—and he adored the rarer varieties such as diamond willow and myrtle wood, and the exotic hardiness of teak and mahogany. Most of all, the thing he loved was to bring out the hidden beauty of his material, polishing and polishing his finishes until they yielded up all the wood's inner secrets, becoming like rich dark mirrors in which one could see one's face.

No longer, of course, did Simon seriously contemplate building a stairway to the sky. But with each article of furniture he created he found himself thinking—not quite deliberately, perhaps, but in spite of himself—*I want this piece to be worthy of being placed in the mansions of heaven.* And like all expert craftsmen, like all artists, he continually fell short of his mark.

Nevertheless, by the time he was thirty, Simon Cyr was as famous as a cabinetmaker could be. He could command any price for his work, and people spoke his name in the same breath as that of Chippendale or Sheraton. And yet, it so happened that just then, at this pinnacle of success, Simon's father took ill very suddenly and died, leaving his one son the sole surviving member of the family. All at once the illustrious young man's career ground to a halt. For, unable even to contemplate proceeding with normal funeral arrangements, Simon found himself seized by a peculiar obsession to build the most beautiful of coffins for his father's remains.

Therefore for weeks, while the body of the old man sat on a slab in the morgue, the son locked himself in his shop and sweated and slaved to come up with a worthy design. But somehow the task eluded him. In a kind of hypnotic frenzy, he took to reading voraciously about the burial practices of ancient and primitive cultures, about the tombs of the Incas and the great Pharaohs. Many peoples, it appeared, had believed literally that material goods might accompany the dead on their journey into the next life. Countless stunning masterpieces had been fashioned solely and deliberately for the purpose of immediate burial and export to heaven. Still, Simon wondered: How was it possible for even the finest artist to create something marvelous and sublime enough for such a purpose? And what if (the question began to gnaw at him) there were no other world at all? What was the sense in making beautiful things if only to hide them in the ground? Or what, really, was the point of making beautiful things at all?

With pitiful irony Simon recalled his own dictum: that a true masterpiece should be capable of bearing a man's weight. Yet what if a man's weight were ultimately nothing but deadweight? What then?

Suddenly, everything that Simon had been seeking to accomplish in his life seemed futile. Worse than futile, it looked insane. For if a living human being could be turned overnight into a shell, a nonentity, then what could be said for the work of his hands? As much as he had been aware of the plain facts about death, never before had Simon been so gripped by its reality. The thing itself was brutally startling, paralyzing, almost as if this were not just his father who had died, but himself.

No, he concluded finally: the central mystery of things could not be unlocked by art. Cabinetmaking was after all no loftier a pursuit than carpentry, and carpentry was no better than digging ditches, or picking pockets, or drinking oneself to death.

Driven to despair by such thoughts, Simon was sitting one day with a bottle of wine on the steps of his father's workshop, utterly despondent, brooding amidst memories and broken dreams, when all at once a peculiar awareness came over him that something was about to happen. All morning the atmosphere had been dense, muggy, almost yellow. But now the yellow turned to black as a great cloud with a nose and belly like a shark came sweeping overhead dragging dark, lashing sheets of rain. The hair on the back of Simon's neck stood straight out. And as the first bolt of lightning split the sky wide open, in the ensuing peal of thunder he clearly heard his father speak to him, uttering again the familiar words—*Simon, do you hear? Do you hear, Simon? They're moving furniture upstairs!*

Just then, glancing up over the steep roof of the neighboring church that was like a pale ghostship riding the storm, the young man caught sight of a single bolt of lightning illuminating the tall steeple, just as though aimed directly at its peak. For seconds the entire building, shivering under splintering cascades of light, looked ready to burst its seams and explode into flames. But the silver steeple stood firm, pointing defiantly to the top of the sky and gleaming more brilliantly than the lightning itself. Indeed, like a dazzling sword it seemed to answer all the wrath of the heavens with a challenge of undaunted, unshakable stability.

This experience branded itself so deeply into Simon Cyr's mind, that as he reflected upon it during the months that followed, he arrived gradually at a radical conclusion: He would completely abandon his secular career, and from thenceforth he would work only for the Church. He would dedicate all his art to the glory of God.

That is the only way, he told himself, to make things that will be worthy of heaven. That is the way to transcend the world.

Of course, the days were long gone in which the Church had been the foremost patron of the arts. And while Simon had previously tried his hand at ecclesiastical furnishings, he had found the work distasteful, inhibiting to the free play of his imagination. Now, however, he threw himself afresh into the study of contemporary church architecture and cabinetry. For a year he did nothing but read and think and travel. And then he began to build: lecterns, prayer desks, communion rails, and row upon row of pews and choir stalls. He made pulpits of stained glass, lit from the inside. For a baptistry he carved praying hands rising twenty feet high like the wings of an angel, and with steps leading up to the font. A rood screen or a reredos by Cyr was like a forest of poplar shimmering in sunlight, and his massive altars floated and soared as though defying gravity.

Years later, this ecclesiastical phase of Simon's career would be hailed by many as the period of his greatest work. Yet for the artist himself, as time wore on, there came an increasingly nagging awareness that something was lacking. For while he would begin a project with great gusto, he always seemed to end in a mood of frustrated fatigue and defeat. His finished works oppressed him; never were they quite what he had envisioned. Though the world praised them, he himself knew too well their flaws. Perfectionism tortured him. His moods grew blacker and blacker, and with each depression he had the feeling of falling into a deep gloomy pit from which he would have to climb painfully up and out before he could again commence work.

And so the question kept plaguing him: Why work at all, if it only destroyed him? Once more there came to mind his childhood dream of a stairway to heaven, a stairway of such light and grace that merely to look upon it would lift one beyond the world, far above the realm of man's bleak and painful struggle. Yet was not the very idea of such a stairway but a mocking illusion? Even as a mere symbol, was it not a lie? Nevertheless, the image persisted. The dream turned into a haunting.

In the end Simon could no longer continue with his work. The joy was gone out of it, and he did not know where to find it again. The Church, particularly, depressed him beyond words, and he came to loathe it for having bled him of all his creative energy. Had he not offered his life's work, all of his very best, to God? And now God had taken it away from him.

Retiring to a foreign country, then, Simon lived alone in a one-room cabin deep in a forest, where he reverted to making the simplest, plainest articles of furniture. He worked only to keep himself occupied. No more gleaming finishes now, no more elaborate arabesques. These pieces were mere sticks, mere objects for sitting on, for eating from, for storing things in. From striving to make furniture that would be worthy of heaven, the master artisan now did a complete about-face, and sought only to make things fit for earth. Yet even here, he felt in his heart, he failed dismally. For everything he touched was smirched and bleared with agonizing self-consciousness.

Eventually he reached the point where he refused even to sell his work, and instead gave it away free to the poor. But it made no difference, for rich collectors came along and snapped up his pieces, praising them to the skies for their rustic simplicity, their purity of line, their amazing economy of material, and so on. Simon Cyr, it appeared, had no choice but to be a great artist. And so, with his dreams changed to hauntings and his gift turned into a curse, the empty weight of mastery hung about his neck like a millstone.

In the final years of his life he made nothing at all. Living as simply as he could, both outwardly and inwardly, he determined in his mind never again to strive after anything. Nevertheless, since it was in a man's nature to strive, in seeking to give it up he found only that his yearning was diverted into another channel, toward the one goal which was most elusive of all: peace.

One day, as a very old man, Simon was out walking in the beautiful forest of tall firs and hemlock that surrounded his hermitage. These were the tallest, straightest trees he had ever seen anywhere, their slender, waving tops distant as memories and all but disappearing in the high and empty blue. The day could not have been more lovely. Sunlight fell like golden rain through the cool canopy of branches. Could any man-made cathedral, mused the old master, boast a more glorious clerestory?

Simon loved this forest, yet at the same time it filled him with a strange sadness, for he knew that even nature, mysteriously, was flawed. Was God Himself incapable of making anything perfect? Often in gazing at the trees, all he could think about was this: that even though these living towers of grace thrust straight upwards, veering barely an inch to the left or to the right, still they could not begin to bridge the impossible distance between earth and heaven. Let them go on forever, he thought; what difference would it make? The very stars fell short.

So as Simon walked, he brooded, retracing the shambles of his career and ruing the foolishness of all his lofty aspirations. With all his art and craft, he could never take two sticks and put them together in such a way as to be worthy of heaven—nor even of earth! Yet it happened on this day that just at the moment he had this thought, he chanced to look down at his feet, and noticed two branches lying there. Possessed by a curious impulse, he stooped down, and, with a single movement, placed one branch, the shorter one, across the other at right angles. Then kneeling on the needle-bedded ground he stared at the figure of a cross he had made. And he found himself recalling the incident from years before in which he had seen his village church dramatically illuminated in a flash of lightning. Once again he was there, and again he saw the tall silver steeple standing against the fulminating sky like a refulgent sword. And then he saw what he had not really seen before—the object that was on top of the steeple.

Why did this object suddenly stir such pangs of strange joy within him? Immediately he recalled his old motto: "A true masterpiece should be capable of bearing a man's weight." Why, all at once, was the thought of this moving him to tears?

Just then Simon felt a stab of pain surging through his chest like a fork of lightning, and right on its heels (though there was not a cloud in the sky) came a stupendous peal of thunder that rolled all around the cavern of his head, and the sound of this thunder was like a voice calling to him, saying— *Simon! Do you hear? Do you hear the furniture moving upstairs? It's being moved for you!*

The two woodcutters who stumbled across Simon Cyr's body in the forest the following day did not even notice the incomparable masterpiece lying on the ground at his feet. The artist's last statement, it was a work of perfect artlessness. And no one ever realized that here, hidden on the forest floor, in this simple ladder with just one rung, lay the stairway to heaven.

* * *

I tell you the truth, you shall see heaven open, and the angels of God ascending and descending on the Son of Man.
John 1:51

The Golden Meteor

"GRANDAD?"

"Yes, Adam?"

"Will you tell me a story?"

"I'd love to. What sort of story did you have in mind?"

"I don't know. Isn't that up to you?"

"I suppose. But maybe you could help me to get started. Any suggestions? Just say the first thing that pops into your head."

"Well, let's see ... Last night, after supper, I heard you and Grandma talking about the first people in the world. Could you maybe tell me a story about them?"

"Why sure, Adam. That makes a good story. In fact, it's one of my favorites. Why don't you pull up a chair over here by the fire, so we can sit and watch the flames together as we talk?"

"Okay."

"Great. Now: Have a good look at the fire. Do you see anything in there?"

"What do you mean?"

"Any shapes? Any creatures?"

"Sure—all kinds!"

"Like what?"

"Well: there's a big tall ship ... a lion ... a galloping horse ... trees ..."

"Good. And all those things live in a world filled with fire, right?"

"Right."

"And all the shapes have that same rich, golden color the fire has, don't they?"

"Yes."

"Beautiful and mysterious?"

"Mm-hm."

"Well, Adam, believe it or not, that's the way everything was in the very beginning. Absolutely everything. The entire universe, from top to bottom and inside out, was filled with fire, dazzling and golden, and everywhere you looked things were leaping and dancing with flames. But do you know what else?"

"What?"

"Nothing ever got burned up."

"No?"

"No. In fact, nothing even got singed. And I'll tell you why: In those days the fire was a cool, comfortable sort of fire. It was the kind of fire you could touch without getting hurt. The kind you could actually walk around in and breathe, just like air."

"No kidding?"

"No kidding. And not only that, but back then this entire earth of ours was made out of solid gold."

"Really?"

"Yes. The whole world, and everything in it—all of it was pure gold. Sort of like this ring I'm wearing, only infinitely purer, and filled with fire. Do you remember that beach we walked on last summer, with golden sand as far as the eye could see?"

"Sure."

"Well, it was all like that, just like that beach in a blazing sunset. Only the sand didn't just *look* like gold, it *was* gold. And it didn't just *look* like it was on fire, it *was* on fire. And wherever there were pebbles, they were all solid gold nuggets, each one with a tiny bonfire nestled inside it. You could pick them up in handfuls and sift them through your fingers."

"Wow!"

"The mountains were pure gold too, clear as the sky and laced with fire, and the very waves of the ocean were molten and flaming. Even the clouds were like finely spun golden wool shot through with lightning, and the trees were gold leaf, and the birds were little flecks of fiery gold soaring on the glittering wind ..."

"But Grandad?"

"Mm?"

"Can I say something?"

"What is it, Adam?"

"It's just that ... well, I don't know whether I would like all of that."

"Oh? How do you mean?"

"Well, wouldn't it get kind of boring after a while? I mean, all that gold all over the place? To me it sounds too much like this story we read in school, about this king with a golden touch ..."

"King Midas?"

"That's him. Everything he touched turned to gold, right? But what good did it do him? Sure, at first he thought it was great. But after a while it wasn't so much fun anymore. It was like everything sort of turned dead in his hands. He couldn't even eat! How can you eat a golden egg?"

"Yes, I see what you mean. That's very perceptive, Adam. And you're right, it's an important story. But you know, for a little boy you sometimes have such a literal mind! Naturally nobody wants to be smothered in gold. But the gold I'm talking about—it wasn't gold as we know it. Not at all. It wasn't the cold, lifeless, metallic rock that ruined King Midas, and that people still grovel and kill for. Oh no, the stuff I'm talking about was far more precious than that! Because, you see, it was something alive. Even the animals were made of it, of this pure molten golden stuff that flowed and breathed and leaped and danced. And remember, too, it was a substance so incorruptible that fire could be contained inside it without burning, melting, or even scorching it. Compared with that, this ring I'm wearing would have looked like a lead washer. And it would have burned up like a toothpick. Do you see what I mean?"

"Maybe."

"Or if you want to think of it a different way, it was more that things had a sort of golden *quality* to them, a luster of holiness and eternity, a kind of shining aura that went right clear through to the very heart of all things. In other words: Everything was positively wonderful and perfect, just the way it was meant to be all along."

"And what about the people?"

"Oh yes, the people. Well, there were just two of them to begin with. A man and a woman. The first people in the world."

"Not a boy and a girl?"

"Say, I hadn't thought of that! But now that you mention it, they must have started off that way. Yet when they got older, something happened that made things not so wonderful and perfect anymore."

"Something bad?"

"Something terrible. It happened this way. The woman—or let's call her a girl—was out walking one morning on one of the beaches. It was a beautiful fine day, just like all the days back then, with everything golden and fiery and glorious like an all-day-long sunset. And the beach was loaded with gold nuggets, miles and miles of them. Not that they all looked the same, mind you, nor were even the same color exactly. But what I mean is—every single pebble the girl laid eyes on was infinitely precious. And every grain of sand, every drop of water, and every glint of fire in every drop. Just close your eyes and try to imagine it."

"So this girl, did she collect some of the nuggets to take home with her?"

"Adam, think for a minute: What would have been the point of that? When there is gold everywhere, do you need to take it home and stuff it away in your drawer?"

"I guess not."

"I'll tell you what did happen, though. All of a sudden, the girl caught sight of something she had never seen before. Something that wasn't gold. It was just sitting there in the middle of the beach, and she couldn't help but notice it because it was black. Pitch-black it was, like a hunk of coal. It seemed dreadfully out of place there on the golden beach. It was just an ugly, lump-shaped thing, like a toad, but it was the only coal-black object the girl had ever laid eyes on in her life. And so you know what?"

"What?"

"She wanted it. Or to use a grown-up word, she coveted it. Just like you said, she wanted to take it home with her—even though it was all lumpy and ugly like a toad, and even though when she picked the thing up she realized it was covered with greasy soot. For to her, finding a lump of coal was something like you or me finding a gold nugget. Just because it was so unusual, you see. So for a moment it didn't matter that all the world, and even she herself, was pure 24-karat gold, sparkling as diamonds and so perfect that it couldn't possibly be any better. Instead, when the girl saw that piece of coal for the first time—ugly and dirty as it was—suddenly everything else didn't look so interesting anymore. Especially when she discovered that whenever she touched the coal, or rubbed it, the black stuff smudged off onto her hands. For some reason she found this terrifically fascinating, and she began making black marks all over her body."

"Like Indian war paint?"

"Exactly. Except in those days there was no such thing as war, and so it didn't make much sense to be dressing up as though there were, did it? Nevertheless, the girl was so thrilled with her rare discovery that immediately she went off to find the boy and tell him all about it. And can you guess what happened next?"

"Let me see ... With all those black smudges on her body, the girl looked so scary and ugly that the boy ran away from her?"

"Ha! That would have been the sensible thing to do! But no, I'm afraid you're wrong. Actually the boy was attracted to the coal just as much as the girl had been, and before long he too was covered with black soot from head to toe. It was just like kids playing in the mud, you know, and getting their brand-new Sunday clothes all dirty. And once they themselves were a mess, they began tracking the mud everywhere they went, and smearing the black on everything else around them—on rocks, trees, animals, even on the sky."

"Really?"

"Sure. Don't you remember when you wrote with crayon all over your mom's living room walls?"

"Oh yeah."

"It was like that. Some people even say this may have been the beginning of writing—but that's another whole story. Anyway, I suppose they just got all caught up in the idea of somehow changing the world, altering it according to their own fancy. It was exciting, you see, to think that they might put something into the world that hadn't ever been there before—even if it was something bad."

"But Grandad?"

"Yes, Adam?"

"If the whole world in the beginning was made of solid gold, like you said, then where did that lump of coal come from?"

"Well, Adam, that's a very good question, and I'm not sure there's a simple answer to it. But you remember the story of the littlest angel, the one who fell to earth? Maybe it was like that. Maybe the coal was really a piece of gold that had somehow lost its fire. And without fire, coal is useless, isn't it? Worse than useless, all it can do is to put black smudges on everything it touches, rubbing out the gold and making it harder and harder for people to appreciate, or even to know about, the beautiful mystery of the fire with which all things were filled at the very beginning.

"Well, I know that doesn't entirely answer your question. But maybe it's one of those things that the more you think about, the more it drives you crazy. Because that's exactly what happened to the first boy and girl: Suddenly all they could think about was black—wondering what black was, where it came from, whether there might be more of it to be found, and so on. And just thinking about black, you see, had a way of spoiling all the beauty of the gold. In fact, it was as if they couldn't see the gold anymore. They only had eyes for black. And even when they did chance to notice a glimmer of gold, their automatic response was to cover it up with soot, almost as though they couldn't stand the brightness of it, or as though the brightness looked dull and unappealing to them. It was like a kind of sickness, a coal-rush fever."

"But what happened when their little hunk of coal got used up?"

"It never did. There were the occasional times when they would wake up and realize—like coming out of a bad dream—just what a terrible mess they were making of the world, painting it all black. And then they would try to get rid of the coal, throwing it away as far as they could. But wherever they threw it, it simply shattered into a thousand pieces, each one the same size as the original. Even when they went down to the beach and hurled the thing out into the sea with all their might, it just stained the water like dye and then came rolling back to them, wave upon wave. So once the black got started, there was no stopping it. Gradually all the fire began to go out in the world, as the golden luster of all its glorious vessels became tarnished. And so the world grew cold—so cold, in fact, that icicles began to form in people's hearts. Their every movement became full of pain, just as though they'd swallowed swords, and before long shivering was second nature to them. At the same time, a dense, sooty darkness had begun to spread over the entire land, a darkness so thick you could feel it. You could reach out and touch this darkness the way you touch a wall, and rub it between your fingers like dust. By the time the boy and girl grew up and had children of their own, things had grown so bad that even at high noon the world was dark as night."

"Really? And what about at night?"

"Night was like drowning in ink. You couldn't see your hand in front of your face. By that stage, of course, people were beginning to realize that gold was something very precious after all, and greatly to be desired. In fact, you couldn't do a thing without it! But the trouble was, there was less and less real gold to be found, and none of it was pure anymore, and so all it did was cause a lot of hard feelings, strife, and eventually wars. I suppose it was something like the way the world thinks of oil today. So people went to the ends of the earth to find gold—but how can you even begin to look for something when it's always night? Here and there you could see a sort of dim golden glow. But it was only a hint, nothing certain. And always far off in the distance, beyond the horizon.

"Well, the earth grew colder and colder and darker and darker, as more and more people filled it. The original parents lived for a long, long time, and the older they got the more they loved to tell stories to their children and grandchildren about the way things used to be—just as I'm telling you now— stories about all the lovely gold and the glorious fire back in the very beginning. But you know, Adam, people who have never seen true fire or real gold find it very difficult to believe that such marvelous things, such pure things, could actually have existed, or that the world was once really and truly like that. Don't you find it hard to believe?"

"A little."

"I do too, to be honest. But that doesn't change the fact that it really was so. People know, you see, deep down, that there's something dreadfully wrong with life the way it is. Even in broad daylight, on a sunny day, we can feel surrounded by darkness. And in our hearts we shiver, as if we're cold inside. Really it's fear—but what are we afraid of? Somehow we can't seem to put our finger on exactly what the problem is, or even how to talk about it. And that's why we need stories—to help us talk about such things. It's also why storytelling is best done around a fire. The fire warms us, you see, and helps to remind us of the true fire that's missing from the world, which is basically what stories are about."

"All stories?"

"Yes. Every story you've ever heard, if you think about it carefully, has the same theme. Because there is really only one story worth telling, and all the others are just variations on it."

"What is the one story?"

"I'm telling it to you right now. At least, we're getting awfully close to it. But first let me finish with the part about the gold and the fire, because next comes my favorite bit—about the Golden Meteor."

"The Golden Meteor?"

"Yes. It's the really good part of the story."

"Is a meteor like a falling star?"

"That's right. Something that comes blazing down out of heaven to earth, lighting up the whole night sky and leaving a gorgeous trail."

"Same as a comet?"

"Not exactly. Because a meteor enters the earth's atmosphere, whereas a comet doesn't. But you're thinking of Halley's Comet, aren't you?"

"Yeah. It wasn't much to look at."

"You're right. Everybody thought it was going to be a lot more spectacular than it was. But do you recall what your dad said that night in December, just after Christmas, when we were all huddled out there on that country road in the freezing cold, passing the binoculars back and forth and trying to figure out if that fuzzy little speck of lint up there in the sky could really be the famous Halley's Comet? The thing that was so fascinating about this obscure object, commented your dad, was just the fact that it had come from *so far away*! Human beings, he said, have a kind of cosmic loneliness, an enormous longing simply to be *visited*—to be visited by something from beyond earth, something truly different from ourselves. That's what science fiction is all about. And religion too, as it happens. That's the real reason why we were all so vastly disappointed in Halley's Comet: the Big Visit we were expecting didn't quite come off.

"But this is precisely where the Golden Meteor fits in, you see. Because as the world grew colder and darker as all the fire went out of it, and people despaired of the idea of ever finding real gold on the earth again, they began to be aware of this deep yearning of theirs to be visited. And the story came to be told of a great chunk of solid gold from outer space that one day would come hurtling down through the atmosphere, blazing an immaculate trail across the sooty sky, so bright and pure that everything it touched would be illuminated, instantly changed into gold, and filled with fire once again— just the way that one single piece of coal had turned everything black. The day was coming, went the story, when a brand new Golden Age would dawn, and cold and darkness would be banished forever. The Golden Meteor would light up everything."

"So when will it happen, Grandad? When will the Golden Meteor come?"

"But don't you know, Adam? Haven't you heard? The great secret is—the Golden Meteor has come already!"

"What?!"

"That's right, it's already here. In fact, every year at Christmas time we celebrate its coming."

"Christmas? I don't get it ..."

"All that decorating with lights, and giving of gifts, and feasting and merriment? And singing songs about 'star of wonder, star of might, star with royal beauty bright'? Don't you see? It's all meant to celebrate the fact that the great Golden Meteor has come bursting into the world, and its fire has already been kindled in our dark lives, and will never go out again."

"But Grandad? If what you're saying is true, then why hasn't everything been changed into gold? Instantly, like you said?"

"Well, Adam, once again that's a very good question. I've spent considerable time scratching my own head over it. But I think one answer might be that this Golden Meteor, looking at it from the outside, can seem a bit like Halley's Comet. That is, it might not look quite as spectacular as everyone expects it to be, and on that account alone a lot of people may have missed it. For as strange as this might sound, the great Golden Meteor can be right under a person's nose, and he won't be able to see it.

The Golden Meteor

"But I think there's another reason, too, why all the world hasn't been set on fire yet, and that's because everything has to be touched first, or illuminated. And it all has to be touched not just on the surface, but through and through. Everything has to come into the light. That takes time, lots and lots of time. When the true gold from heaven touches a person, it's true that it changes him instantly. But then that person has to go and touch someone else. I have to touch you, and you have to touch me back, and then we both have to touch your mom and dad, and so on. Otherwise, the fire never gets very bright. For the secret of building a fire, as my own grandfather used to tell me, is very simple: it's just one log up against another. But believe it or not, Adam, the odd thing is that not everybody wants to be touched like that. Not everybody wants to be refined into gold."

"Grandad?"

"Yes, Adam?"

"I think maybe I know why not."

"Oh? And why is that?"

"Well, the whole thing just sounds sort of weird. I mean, let's say it happened to me. How would I do anything anymore, all set on fire and turned into gold like that?"

"Ah, there you go again! You know what, Adam? You're still thinking about King Midas. You're afraid of being zapped and turned into a statue or something. But don't you remember what I said, about this gold being different? It's exactly the reverse of the King Midas story, because this is *living* gold. When the Golden Meteor touches you, you don't go dead like a statue. Instead, you realize you've been a statue all along, and you wake up! The fire goes pouring right into your frozen veins, and you come alive!"

"It's hard to imagine."

"It's impossible to imagine. You can only experience it. But maybe I'm giving you the wrong impression. This isn't something magic I'm talking about. There's no abracadabra here, nothing weird. It's more like ... Well, really the only word for it is *love*. Everything has to be touched and changed by love."

"Grandad? Have you seen this Golden Meteor yourself?"

"Yes, I have."

"And been touched by it? Set on fire?"

"Yes."

"So what does it feel like? Is it like being struck by lightning?"

"Well, some people say it is. But that's not quite the way it happened for me. In my case it was more like walking along a beach that was covered with coal—charred, sooty coal for miles and miles. Even the water was inky black, and the sky too, darker than thunderheads, and hanging so low that I had to stoop and grovel just so I wouldn't bump my fool head on it. The whole scene, if you can picture it, was like some big ugly oil spill, and I was just a seagull stuck in the stuff, every feather mired with grime. And cold! I tell you, I couldn't have been colder if I'd been a walking skeleton, with no flesh at all on my bones. I mean, I'm just giving you a picture of what my life felt like in those days. Inside and outside, everything was cold and black.

"But all at once, in the midst of all that gloom, what do you think happened? I saw a light! A golden light! It wasn't very bright—not at first. Nothing like a bolt of lightning, nor even a shooting star. No, it was more like a tiny, distant candle flame, burning with a warm steady glow there on the dark beach. Burning and burning without going out, without even wavering. So I went toward it—what else was there to do? And you know, the nearer I came to that glowing flame, the brighter it grew. Yet even when I was close enough to actually kneel down beside the light and warm myself, I don't think I realized what it was. I don't think I had any idea that what I was looking at was a piece of gold—real gold. A genuine gold nugget, filled with fire. Imagine, among all that filthy coal—me striking gold!

"Of course, I'd never seen real gold before. And unlike so many other people, I hadn't even been looking for it. I suppose, in a way, it was the furthest thing from my mind. Yet as soon as I picked it up and held it in my hands, right away it began to change me, to warm me, clear through to the inside. And that's when I realized what it was. That's when I knew that I'd found the Golden Meteor! Not because I saw some magnificent fireball blazing across the sky. No, it was just that for the first time in my life I knew that I was touching, and being touched by, something genuine. Here was something *real*! In fact, here was reality itself—something so perfectly pure and true that, like the Alchemists' Stone you may have heard about, it actually had the power to change ordinary rock into gold. It was the Golden Meteor, you see, the true gold come down from heaven: the one thing in all the universe which not only is real itself, but which imparts life and reality to everything else. And here I was holding this life in my hands!"

"Grandad?"

"Yes, Adam?"

"This Golden Meteor—it's Jesus, right?"

"That's right."

"Then why didn't you just tell me so from the beginning?"

"Well, Adam, maybe it's because that's the way I think God likes to tell things. In stories. And maybe it takes a lot of stories before we really begin to get the message. After all, in the Bible He kept on telling people stories for a few thousand years before He finally let us know that every one of them was all about Jesus."

"Grandad?"

"Yes, Adam?"

"You're weird. But I love you."

The Golden Meteor

* ✳ *

The words of the Lord are radiant, giving light to the eyes ... More desirable are they than gold, yea, than much fine gold!
    Psalm 19:8, 10

The Great Author

ONCE NOT SO LONG AGO, in a kingdom quite nearby, there lived a great author who was so famous that he could not walk down the street—any street anywhere in the world—without being instantly recognized by everybody. He was so unbelievably, inexpressibly famous that his name had long ceased to be a household word. For it is one thing to be so famous that everyone is talking about you, but it is something else again when your very name is so fraught with awe that no one dares speak it except in hushed and furtive tones.

It was most curious, this guardedness surrounding the mere mention of the author's name. People got around it by referring to him only obliquely and impersonally, employing various popular epithets such as The Master, The Great Author, or even simply The Author. And although it was true that many liked to discuss The Great Author's books (while many more liked to speculate about his private life), the odd fact was that in spite of all this talk, there were few who had actually read his work for themselves.

Whenever The Great Author made one of his rare public appearances, naturally there were many different reactions to him. Some people fainted dead away at his mere presence. Others ran after him and stepped over one another just trying to touch him. There were also those who pretended not to care anything at all about him, turning up their noses as he passed, or busying themselves with other things. And then, not so surprisingly, there were the sort of people who actually lay in wait for him, watching for some opportunity to trip him up or even to do away with him. For like every famous person, he had many more enemies than friends.

To The Author himself, all of this was a source of great sadness. For he was the sort of person who would have loved to walk about freely in the world, taking time out to chat informally with everyone from the washerwoman to the elevator operator. But increasingly, this sort of life was denied him. The more his fame grew, the more impossible it was for him to show his face without provoking widespread disturbance. Controversy, riots, trouble of all sorts followed in his wake—not because he advocated any of these things in his writings, but only because everyone on earth, from the greatest to the least, was secretly jealous of The Great Author's enormous fame, and every one of them was prepared to go to any lengths in order to grab a piece of it for themselves. Even some of his most devoted fans tended inadvertently to discredit and subvert his reputation. For that is the way it is with fame.

In time, The Great Author had no other choice but to suspend his public appearances altogether. Much as it pained him, he withdrew into seclusion, and for many years his only human contacts were with a small secretarial staff. His detractors, predictably, accused him of living in an ivory tower, cut off from the realities of life. But the books kept appearing, and the writing continued to be more beautiful, more deeply realistic, and more glorious by far than anything else the world had ever seen, so that even in exile The Author's reputation increased staggeringly. His books were perennial best-sellers, and there was hardly a house anywhere that did not have his Collected Works (often in several different editions) sitting on the bookshelf. He was revered equally by common people and by scholars, so that it actually became something of an insult to label his writing as "great literature," since it so obviously was much more than that. His words were like the very breath of life.

As the years of his involuntary exile dragged on, eventually a rumor got abroad that The Great Author must have died. Some even speculated that, like the figures in the pages of his own books, he himself might be a fictitious character.

"How could such a person really exist?" asked the public. "He's too prodigious to be believed."

"And surely such an awesome and prolific range of work," pointed out many, "could not possibly have been produced by one single artist."

Where, then, had the books come from? The theory arose that they had probably had some sort of folk origin. Scholars detected clear textual evidence that scores of anonymous editors had been involved in the compilation of the works. Although this theory had its problems, one thing appeared more and more certain: that it was ridiculous to believe the books had all been authored by a single Great Master whose very existence no one seemed able to prove.

"After all," the people said, "nobody's actually seen this fellow for years. If he really exists, let him come down from his ivory tower and show himself."

Accordingly, even though his writing was there in black and white for all to see, the writer himself became a thing of legend, a being too fabulous to be real. It seemed that the greater his notoriety, the deeper grew his enforced separation from the world. The more his work was venerated, the more the person behind the veneration had to be kept at arm's length, as if at all costs to prevent him from entering ordinary life and being contaminated. In time The Author even had to dismiss his secretarial staff, since by that point he was so famous that nobody could quite relate to him anymore.

To The Author himself, sequestered like a leper, all cf this trumped-up mystification was profoundly painful. Not the sort of a fellow to mope around in loneliness and self-pity, nevertheless he longed to be a part of the world, to have friends, to socialize, and even to marry. For by nature he was anything but a hermit, and what others referred to as his ivory tower was to him a dark dungeon. To his mind, it would have been heaven just to be able to walk out in broad daylight without stirring up mayhem.

And so it was that in near-desperation he hit upon a radical plan:

In a tiny village close by there happened to live a slave girl, severely oppressed and in a hopeless condition. The Author had often noticed her on his secret walks, and his heart had gone out to her. So one night in winter he came knocking at her door, introduced himself, and made her a proposal of marriage! So taken aback was the girl that it was months before The Author could convince her that his intentions were completely honorable. But he was patient, and eventually she believed him and accepted his offer. Immediately her freedom was purchased, and there followed a great wedding celebration attended by all her relatives.

It was the first time in years that The Great Author had been able to sit down and rub shoulders with average folk, and at long last he was in his element. Just as he had hoped, the wedding was the beginning of a bridge for him into ordinary life. (For even though the whole world might be busy puffing a fellow up, his own relatives could always be counted on to cut him down to size.) Here, at least, was a group of people who accepted The Great Author as being one blood with themselves.

The honeymoon, nevertheless, was short-lived. For in no time at all the relatives took to hounding their famous new kinsman for money and for all sorts of favors, and they were forever wanting him to put in appearances at various functions designed purely for their own social advancement. If in any way he failed to meet such demands, the in-laws would respond by snubbing him.

Even the bride herself, although she was as common as a woman could be, took to putting on airs, jetsetting all over the countryside and entangling herself in no end of mischief. She seemed to take it for granted that she could get away with anything, and the little time she did put in at home she spent chafing and wheedling her husband, or else ignoring him completely. In short she became, like the spouses of so many other famous people, nothing but a notorious socialite, a person famous for no other reason than that she was famous, and especially celebrated for her adulterous affairs. In the end, to no one's surprise, she died a premature and sordid death, leaving her husband right back where he had started.

Meanwhile, debates concerning The Author's true identity had been raging anew. Reports of his appearances in the early days, and throughout the time of his marriage, were taken to be purely fanciful. It was all an elaborate hoax, many said. Would the true Great Author have married a worthless whore? Could his writing be so full of wisdom if the man himself were nothing but a foolish old doter?

Even the books themselves came under fire, as people began wondering aloud whether they really were all that they were cracked up to be. After all, who could pass any final judgment in a matter as subjective as that of literary taste? So it became fashionable to detect flaws in these supposed writings of The Master, and while it was admitted that they surely contained an unusual degree of what might be termed "wisdom" or "truth," it was also cautioned that such things were of a highly relative nature. Truth itself, in the last analysis, was something ineffable and unknowable, and therefore the sort of claims that had once been made for these works were now deemed outrageous. Certainly any statement to the effect that a mere book might contain *the* Truth, or the *only* Truth, had to be severely qualified.

Time passed, and more and more The Great Author yearned to come down from his pedestal. But how? The people themselves kept him up there, pushing him away as if his very genius were like a bad odor, a stench as repugnant to them as that of rotting flesh. They had, in a sense, celebrated The Author to death.

"How strange it is," he lamented, "that here I am writing all these books, in an effort to communicate heart-to-heart with my readers. And yet the books are actually having the effect of distancing me more than ever."

Eventually The Author re-married, once again choosing a common servant girl. But this time the wedding was kept a secret, and the bride and her renowned husband went off together to live in peaceful seclusion. Perhaps the answer, reflected The Author now, was just to settle down and raise a family, to stop producing books for a while, and instead to produce offspring from his own loins. And indeed, when his first son was born, right from the beginning the lad delighted his father's heart, and as he grew up in the father's house he seemed in every way to be the fulfillment of the Great Author's highest expectations. For the boy was, quite simply, the apple of his old man's eye.

When it came time for the child to be educated, he was sent abroad into the world—not to any special private school, but rather to an ordinary public school a long way from home. Even from this distance, however, The Author observed his son's progress with immense and increasing joy. For not only did the boy love his father implicitly and honor him with absolute obedience, but he also shared his father's innermost heart and vision to such an extent that even while the two were apart, they were, for all intents and purposes, one in spirit. In fact, the son actually began living out in flesh the very truth and wisdom of which the father had written in his books. Although he himself would never author a book, by the time he came of age it was perfectly clear that his whole life was being dedicated to the telling of his father's stories, to the teaching of his father's concepts, and to the acting out of his father's message to the world. The Author, for his part, was overjoyed to see that the ideas he had conceived were no longer mere words, but were being fleshed out in real life by his son. Here at last was the elusive link with humanity of which the father had dreamed! The daily life among common people that he himself had been kept from, he now could live out vicariously through his son.

Oddly enough, however, the world's reaction to this parvenu son turned out to be rather different from its reaction to his admittedly more famous father. For while in most circles the old man continued to be regarded quite highly (and this in spite of the fact that a growing number were casting aspersions upon his work), the son, on the other hand, was viewed as a troublemaker, an upstart, just one more in the long string of charlatans who had sought to capitalize on The Master's reputation.

For some reason, the very material that had been so esteemed when it first came out in book form appeared suddenly far too dangerous and radical when presented in the flesh. People would go to extraordinary lengths to find excuses for rejecting this so-called "son" out of hand, claiming not only that he misrepresented his father's ideas, but also that he was not even a true son at all but an impostor, a lunatic, a bastard, and so on. For just as the public's method of dealing with the fame of The Great Author himself had been to glorify him out of reach, so now they dealt with the rising star of the son by disdaining and slandering both him and his cause. Even as they mentioned the name of the father in reverent whispers, the name of the son they spoke in tones ranging all the way from scorn, to open outrage, to cold apathy or shame. Even those who knew and secretly admired him, it seemed, would sooner have been caught dead than let their intimate association with him be made known.

It was no wonder, really, for the son made a practice of standing up in public and coming out with statements that were grossly embarrassing. He would say, for example:

"You people don't want reality—you want books! 'Give us more books,' you cry, 'but don't give us life itself!' You want love and truth to be something you can put between two covers and set on a shelf where it can gather dust. And yet here I am, offering you

The Great Author

real love and truth in the flesh, on behalf of my father whom you claim to revere—but you don't want me!"

Naturally the people took great exception to such scolding, and they were particularly shocked by the son's bold claim, inherent in everything he said, that he himself was the living embodiment of all the father's wisdom. For he went so far as to state: "I am what my father has been writing about all these years. I am The Great Author's message. If you really believed in his greatness, you would also believe in me." With boasts such as these, in spite of widespread public rejection the son's reputation burgeoned alarmingly, until in many people's eyes his glory had begun to rival that of the old man himself.

About this time, a worldwide symposium was organized in honor of The Great Author. From all parts of the globe gathered scholars, teachers, fans, and other writers, and day after day for a solid week papers were delivered, discussions held, and all manner of tribute paid. The son, predictably, had not been invited to this convention, and yet everyone there was speculating as to whether or not he might put in one of his unpredictable appearances. And sure enough, on the very last day at the height of the festivities, who should show up on the mainstage but the only son of the object of all these celebrations? And taking over the microphone, in a loud voice he set about denouncing the entire proceedings, declaring that anyone who truly loved good literature would listen to him, because his words were the exact equivalent of The Great Author's.

"I am the one," he said, "whom by rights you should be exalting with all your papers, your tributes, and indeed your very lives. For unless you honor me, your veneration of my father is nothing but an empty sham."

At this, pandemonium broke out on the convention floor.

"Who does this fellow think he is," shouted the delegates, "barging in here and breaking up our assembly, and claiming to be the equal of The Great Author? Why, he's not even a writer himself! What does he know about good literature? Get him out of here—he's stark raving mad! He's an enemy of the arts!"

At once a group of the loudest radicals went storming right up onto the stage and laid hands upon the son, and ushering him brusquely outside they began beating him up in the back alley. The rest of the mob followed, chanting and cheering them on, and soon reporters had gathered with flashbulbs popping and cameras rolling. Thus in no time the ugly scene, live and in color, was being broadcast all around the world, and people everywhere looked on from their armchairs with benign absorption as the battered body of the son was dragged through the streets and alleyways, mockingly pelted with copies of his own father's books, and finally stuffed ignominiously into a garbage bin in a filthy stairwell, where he was left to die.

Even as these events were unfolding, it so happened that The Great Author himself was clandestinely present in the convention city, and that very moment was watching the televised report from his hotel room. When he saw with his own eyes what the crowd was doing to his son, his heart simply broke. Without any heed for himself or for his own safety, without any of the normal precautions, the distraught father went rushing out of his room undisguised and tore down the hallway. Already in the lobby heads were turning in recognition, and as the famous figure sprinted through the open streets traffic crawled to a halt and thronging multitudes fell in behind him. By the time he had reached the actual site of his son's brutal mauling, the crowd was so thick that it was all he could do to pry his way through them. People tugged at him, pawed him, tore his clothing. But the father pressed forward, broke through their ranks, and finally, catching sight of the tortured body of his only son, he ran like the wind itself into the midst of the garbage heap and fell upon him, throwing his arms around the bleeding flesh and crying aloud like any child.

By that point, quite clearly, the son was already dead—and what a woeful, heart-rending picture they made, the two of them, as tremblingly the famous father cradled in his lap the limp and broken body of his own flesh and blood, sobbing and sobbing as if all his tears might somehow replenish the life that had spilled out from his son's wounds.

Could any sound be more excruciating than that of the incontinent, public weeping of a grown man? And here was the greatest and most honored man of all the earth, dissolved in grief.

"Look how he mourns!" remarked some of the onlookers. "Could it be that everything this lad said about himself was true, and that he really was the son of The Great Author?"

Most, however, remained skeptical. "Nobody has seen The Author for years," they said. "So how do we know this old character kneeling by the body is really he? Besides, would The Master himself break down and cry his heart out in front of the whole world?"

Indeed, this very moment, even as they watched, the old man's familiar appearance seemed to be changing before their eyes, disfigured by the trauma of his loss. For his eyes had grown wide and bright with pain, and the skin shrank tight around his skull. Tears like acid ate crevices down his sunken cheeks, and all his features were twisted in agony. The once noble face, which everyone had known so well and yet no one had quite been able to identify with, appeared now to have been transformed into something as common as clay.

"Look—this fellow's not so great after all!" the people exclaimed. "Where is all his wisdom and grandeur now? Where are his fine-sounding words?

When it comes down to the death of his own little boy, he's no different from any of the rest of us."

"So what are we doing hanging around here?" asked others. "Kids die every day, and parents mourn like it's the end of the world. But it's nothing new. Life goes on. Besides, that son of his was nothing but a little hooligan."

And so the crowd dispersed that day, and the great symposium drew to a close, and The Author was left all alone to do his grieving. When finally he rose to his feet, as evening fell, and went trudging back to the hotel room, no multitudes clamored after him along the way this time, and no one clutched at the hem of his garment. It wasn't only that the people had no interest in a broken man; the plain fact was that hardly anyone recognized him anymore.

Grief changes a person.

As the dust of these events settled, there were only a few who still saw him for what he was: the greatest Author of all time, the undisputed Master, essentially unchanged even in tragedy. These were the same people, in fact, who all along had fully accepted the authenticity of the son, identifying in him the perfect image of his father. It was these few, and these only, who were now able to recognize the father, for these were the ones for whom any amount of trouble—whether grief, pain, mockery, or death itself—could never be enough to conceal the underlying truth of things. So in the ensuing weeks and months these faithful ones sought out The Great Author and gathered around him, until a most surprising thing began to happen. For The Author found that among these followers he was able to relax and be completely himself! He could talk freely with them, enjoy his meals at the same table, and even walk openly with them through the streets. For while these folk continued to revere him even more than they had before, there was now something new that had drawn them all much closer to him—as close, indeed, as if he had been their very own father, or brother.

That something new was his grief. It was the simple humanness of The Author's grief that had finally shattered the strange spell cast over him by fame, bringing to an end his long exile from ordinary life and creating for him a brand new family. Thus the door that had been closed to him all these years had, miraculously, swung open, and at long last he was free to live like anyone else in the world, surrounded by loved ones.

And then another wonderful thing began to happen: New books appeared! New books from The Master's hand! These latest works, moreover, were even more glorious and brilliant than his previous ones had been. For they were all about his son. And where the son had laid down his life to glorify his father, so now the father poured all his energy into glorifying his beloved son. And as more and more people came to read those new books, they too were drawn irresistibly to the father, and yet no longer merely as fans to a celebrity, but rather as children into the warm circle of their very own family. For now they saw the greatness not just of The Author's artistic genius, but of his love, so that never again would this greatness be such as to distance The Master beyond the reach of his readers.

In this way the father's new family grew and grew, and where all else had failed to bridge the impossible gap between The Great Author and his worshipful audience, the death of his only son availed.

* * *

Let us fix our eyes on Jesus, the Author and Perfecter of our faith, who for the joy set before Him endured the cross, scorning its shame, and sat down at the right hand of the throne of God.
    Hebrews 12:2

Christopher
Rainbow

WITH CHRISTOPHER RAINBOW AND ME, right from the start it was one of those stormy romances: on again, off again, on again, off again. So when the news first came out about this new technique that's been discovered for merging two people into one, we simply made up our minds one night, he and I, to throw caution to the winds and give it a try. I guess it just seemed high time for us to take some kind of permanent, irreversible step, and so we thought—well, why not? *Why not go all the way?*

After all, people are always hopping into bed together these days, and it's nothing for couples to shack up. So when this new method of total fusion became available, and we began seeing it advertised all over the place, it just seemed like the natural thing for Christopher and me to do.

Of course, I realize that it must strike many people as shockingly grotesque, the very idea of two separate people being literally melted down into one. But if you stop and think about it, it's really no more peculiar a thing than shaking hands, say, or kissing—to say nothing of making love! I mean, who would ever have thought of such things? No matter how common they may become, the most ordinary gestures of intimacy retain a perpetual savor of strangeness. And ultimately, don't they all point in the same direction, toward deeper and deeper union?

Naturally Christopher and I had a big church ceremony, and I won't go into all the details of that. But the moment itself, that moment when the two of us were standing there hand-in-hand before the altar and then suddenly, physically, were melded together—how can I describe that? Well, one thing I can say is that instead of being inside myself, looking out at Christopher, suddenly I felt that *I was inside Christopher, looking out at myself!* One moment I was minding my own business, more or less, and the next moment I was minding business for Christopher Rainbow.

Looking back on it, I can see that before then, in spite of having a lover and all, really I was still behaving pretty much like my own person: single, autonomous, marching to a private drum. And expecting Christopher just to tag along! It was almost as though I were the only person on earth, lost in my own little dream world. But ever since that mysterious transaction at the altar, like it or not I've found myself living not my own life but Christopher's: doing Christopher's work, thinking Christopher's thoughts, getting used to Christopher's body as being my own body, and trying, however clumsily, to do all things just the way Christopher wants them done. And since there is legally only one living person now in place of two, I even took his full name, first and last, as my own: *Christopher Rainbow.*

My parents, predictably, were outraged. They'd been dead against the thing all along, refusing even to come to the ceremony. But you should have seen them the day Christopher and I walked into their home as one person! I mean, on top of everything else Christopher has this thick foreign accent, which to my ears sounds adorable, but which I know turns a lot of people off. So even before we got in the door my parents heard my familiar voice all mixed up with that alien voice. And as soon as they laid eyes on the face of their dear daughter pressed shamelessly into the face of this foreigner, and saw my lips moving with his in a kind of perpetual osculation—well, they just freaked out. They had no idea who I was anymore, they said, and merely to look at me, all wrapped up in that man, sent shivers up and down their spines.

From the way they carried on you'd have thought I'd been lost to them forever! You'd have thought that getting joined together with a strange man was something unutterably disgusting, even perverted, for a decent woman to do. Well, if it had been anyone else besides Christopher Rainbow, I'm sure I would agree with them. But Christopher just happens to be the soul of decency, the paragon of purity and goodness. How can you argue with true love?

I don't mean to imply that it's all been smooth sailing for Christopher and me. We've had our ups and downs, believe me, and I can't honestly say I don't ever miss myself, the way I used to be. The fact is, I do get frustrated not being able to run my own show. I know it's silly, since there's no going back now. But it's one thing to *be* one with another person, and it's another thing altogether to *function* as one. In the beginning, especially, the two of us weren't coordinated at all, and I'm sure that's partly what put my family off. It was as though I and a perfect stranger had thrown a moth-eaten blanket over our heads and were pretending to be a dancing horse. We kept stepping on toes, getting in each other's way. And we were constantly having these long discussions about how to work things out. My feeling was that the only sane way to operate was on a fifty-fifty basis: half of the time we'd be me, and the other half we'd be him. What could be fairer than that? But Christopher, being from the Old Country, wouldn't hear of it, and seemed determined not just to share my life but to take it over completely.

Even now, there's hardly a day goes by when we don't have to talk this issue through, and sort out what it all means. And again and again Christopher has to explain patiently to me that what actually happened, that moment before the altar when I got joined to him, was that I *died* to my old existence, and a brand new person was formed. Can't I see how preposterous it is, he'll argue, for me to keep on trying to revert to my old independent self, when that self is now nothing but a dead shell? When I don't even have a living body to call my own anymore?

"So what about you?" I'll pout. "It's a two-way street, you know. How come you get off scot-free?"

"Oh, but I don't," he answers simply. "Aren't you forgetting that I died too?"

And at that, the very shadow that crosses his face will steal across mine, and I'll feel my lips begin to tremble just as his do, and in my eyes—which are really *our* eyes—the tears will spring. And then in our heart I'll know that he is right. Then I'll know that fifty-fifty is impossible, and that nothing makes any sense anymore but for the two of us to become totally and unconditionally identified, immolated into one another.

So it hasn't always been easy, living in Christopher Rainbow, or having him living in me. He can be so difficult to figure out sometimes, so full of inconsistencies. I mean, first he'll say one thing, and then he'll say something else that sounds exactly the opposite. Or we'll be on our way to the supper table, for example—and I'll be starving—and suddenly he'll remember that he has to make this important phone call, and the next minute we'll be throwing on our coat and heading out the door to some dire emergency. And right in the middle of that, he's liable to stop and spend some time playing around with the neighborhood kids! That's just the kind of man he is. You never quite know what he's going to do next. And yet somehow he expects me to be able to keep up with all of this, and even to read his mind. Because he's doing it all, remember, inside of me—right inside my mind and body—even though what I want sometimes is just to get on with a few harmless and quite legitimate plans of my own. Like fooling around with some of my old friends, maybe, or sleeping in on a Sunday morning, and so on. I tell you, it can be mighty painful, always being yanked in two directions at once.

But then, I guess the truth of it is that I felt much more like a schizophrenic before meeting Christopher Rainbow than after. For somehow, in spite of everything, I'm more *myself* now than I've ever been. And the better I get to know Christopher on the inside, the more his odd behavior on the outside seems not so crazy or inconsistent anymore, but makes perfect sense to me. You really have to walk around in a person's shoes before you start seeing things their way.

So that's why I can so heartily recommend this new technique of fusing people together, whatever little problems it might create. Mind you, I'd never dream of doing it with anyone except Christopher Rainbow! I mean, getting hooked up like this with the wrong person would be sheer hell.

* * *

On that day you will realize that I am in my Father, and you are in me, and I am in you.
    John 14:20

Jessica and the Talking Tree

WHEN LITTLE JESSICA came home from school saying that a big tree in the park had spoken to her, naturally her parents didn't pay her much heed.

The stories kids dreamed up! They lied as easily as they breathed. Or was it just that the line between reality and fantasy was drawn differently for children? In any case, it was cute the way Jessica's tiny face could screw itself up into a look of such dead seriousness, while spinning a pure cock-and-bull tale.

Three days later, however, the child was still so adamant about the thing that she managed to drag both her mother and her father halfway across town to listen to the tree for themselves. And after that it wasn't long before the old folks changed their tune.

For there was no doubt about it: something *was* going on over there in the shadowy woods, something mighty unusual. Strange rumblings could be heard all the way across the park, and the earth—albeit ever so gently—was trembling. As Mom and Dad drew closer, they saw that a knot of onlookers had gathered at a respectful distance around the base of a big old oak.

The voice appeared to be emanating from somewhere below ground, in the tree's roots, although the trunk and the crown were also involved and seemed to be functioning as a sort of megaphone. Though there was no wind, all the leaves shivered delicately, like resonant membranes, and a few of those in the crowd who had ventured ever so gingerly to touch the rough bark, testified that vibrations could be plainly felt.

Otherwise, just to look at the tree, there was nothing too unusual about it. It was one more among many that had been left standing in a fringe of woods along one side of the open park area. Of course, the more one studied this particular tree, the more it did seem to take on unique and fascinating characteristics. Some people, for example, said that they could see actual words formed in the configuration of twigs and branches, and others even claimed to make out the faces of famous personages. So there was much gesticulating and vehement discussion.

But fundamentally it was the voice, and the voice alone, which drew attention. It was a dark, throaty, growling sort of voice, less like that of a human being than of a large yawning animal—a bear, say, or a lion. Yet at the same time, it was quite clear that there was something highly sophisticated about it. The tree was not producing mere brutish sounds, but was uttering distinct syllables that flowed together unmistakably into human-sounding language. At least, it was an articulate language of some sort—whether anthropomorphic, arboreal, or angelic.

As for the interpretation of the language, that remained a mystery. For while some in the crowd claimed it reminded them of the Old Country dialects of their grandparents, and swore they could pick out familiar phrases here and there, the truth was that no one could really make head nor tail of what the tree might be saying.

"It's no great wonder," remarked one man. "Should a tree be expected to speak in English?"

"But if it really wanted to communicate with us," observed Jessica's mother, "you'd think it could make itself plainer."

"That's what I say!" chimed in another woman. "Why beat about the bush?"

One observer, who happened to be the chief of the local Indian band, appeared vastly amused by all this commotion. "Are you folks really so surprised that a tree should talk?" he kept saying. "Why, trees have spoken to the Indian for hundreds of years! But the white man has never listened to the Indian, so why should he bother with trees?"

Meanwhile, Jessica's father, being Mayor of the town, took matters quickly in hand and began calling in experts. In no time teams of botanists, biochemists, and even anthropologists were arriving from the university, together with every imaginable breed of linguist: polyglot, grammarian, philologist, the scholar of ancient tongues, all the way to the theologian specializing in ecstatic utterances. There was even the odd astronomer devoted to the detection of extraterrestrial signals, and a husband-and-wife team considered the world's foremost authorities on communication with plants.

All these descended upon the talking oak and subjected it to a battery of investigations. For a while the tree held more wires than branches, and there was hardly a leaf or a square inch of bark that was not at one time or another attached to an electrode. Indeed, above the constant whirr of all the elaborate machinery, the voice itself was often difficult to distinguish. Nevertheless, after months of the most intense and invasive study, still no plausible explanation could be found for the speech phenomenon (although many an elegant theory was promulgated, and many a paper published), and neither could any of the experts convincingly crack the code of the cryptic language.

By this time the site had also attracted its share of oddballs, curiosity seekers, and occultists, and there arose a welter of mystical interpretations of the tree's pronouncements. Every day self-appointed prophets stood on the town's street corners and proclaimed various messages in the tree's name. Tracts were handed out, strange rituals performed, and photographs and recordings were sold, venerated, and endlessly analyzed.

Still the old oak continued to pour forth speech—sometimes in the stentorian tones of public oration, other times in the faintest of whispers, occasionally even in song. Quiet for hours, days, or occasionally weeks at a stretch, time and again the voice would suddenly break forth in the most surprising ways.

Since no one was capable of predicting when or how the tree might speak, always there was a crowd gathered in the park, at all hours of the day or night. Even those who made no great claim to comprehend the message seemed nevertheless to draw a deep, inscrutable satisfaction merely from listening. Thousands camped out on the grass, and Jessica's father finally had to give up on trying to have transients evicted.

A more serious problem arose, however, when bits of the talking tree's bark began to be revered as icons. Despite the frenzied protection of scholars and technicians, and despite even the periodic earth tremors, whole strips of bark were being peeled away by the rabble, until in places the moist white flesh of the sapwood was exposed. Before long it became abundantly clear that if something were not done,

the entire tree stood in danger of being destroyed—
and that, ironically, by the very devotees who
cherished it most highly.

Once again, the Mayor took swift action. By-laws
were rammed through, forbidding anyone to touch or
even to come near the priceless tree. Imposing
barbed wire fences were erected around it, and stern
signs posted. In further steps, the town launched a
beautification program for the park, and glossy
tourist brochures appeared hailing the district as
Home of the Famous Talking Tree.

Mysteriously, the more such measures were
enacted, the more the tree began to grow laconic. Its
silences became longer and longer, to the point
where even when it did speak, the voice tended to be
so quiet that it was difficult to be sure whether the
big oak were really and truly verbalizing, or whether
the hushed whisperings might not be just the sighing
of wind among the leaves. The prodigy
deteriorated to the point where pilgrims to the site
were considered most fortunate if they managed to
catch even one or two words, and most had to be
content simply to absorb the reminiscences of the
local townspeople.

In time, as many of the more reputable scientists
dispersed, a climate of skepticism set in. Definite
camps arose: those who insisted that the tree had
really spoken, and still spoke; those who openly
scoffed at any such suggestion; those who attempted
a compromise by saying that while the tree perhaps

had spoken at one time, it did so no longer; those who flatly refused to discuss the subject at all; those who admitted that some sort of "noise" may well have been produced, but that uninterpretable sounds could not properly be construed as a language, nor even as a voice; and so on.

But the real trouble erupted when the rumor started circulating that the leaves of the talking oak were effective for producing miraculous cures. At first, people were content to gather up the few dead leaves (the crumbs under the table, as it were) that chanced to fall outside the double enclosure of barbed wire. But when a series of particularly spectacular healings was reported, the crowds grew more aggressive. Profiteers took to climbing over the fences at night and harvesting whole bushel baskets of the living foliage.

In short order the great tree was all but denuded, and even two or three of the lower limbs were sawn off. Thus the once stately and beautiful oak became an eyesore, a grim gibbet at the height of summer. Though guards were posted around the clock, the physical abuses continued and waxed more violent. One night two town policemen were murdered at the site, and when the armed forces' riot squad was called in, a number of bystanders were trampled to death.

There ensued a chaotic week of skirmishes, demonstrations, looting, and general mayhem. The tree itself, stripped now of its majesty, uttered not a single word either in protest or self-defense, but simply stood its ground, silent as any board of lumber. Not even the wind made the faintest rustle anymore among its black, naked branches. Indeed, as even the most ardent believers were now heard to mutter, if ever there had been any supernatural voice, it must have long since died away, or else had retreated into so infinitely soft a whisper as to be indistinguishable by human ears. Naturally, no more miraculous healings were reported during this period, and most reached the conclusion that the former rumors had been greatly exaggerated.

Finally, in an all-night emergency session, the Mayor and his Council came to grips with the painfully obvious reality confronting them: that their beloved tree, having in the long run brought nothing but grief to their peaceful little community, was really more trouble than it was worth—and especially now that its amazing tongue had apparently been silenced. The thing wasn't even much to look at anymore, and there was good reason to question whether this pitiful, leafless hulk could ever again recover from its grievous wounds.

Accordingly, it was a somber group of Town Fathers who eventually decided, regretfully but unanimously, that the best and safest course at this point would be simply to cut the thing down and be done with it. Anticipating resistance to such a drastic step, Council immediately called together the

Municipal Works Crew and issued the dread order, so that that very night, well before dawn, the buzz-saws and the bulldozers swung into action. But would it really be that simple, some councilors wondered? Could order be secured merely by eliminating a half-dead hunk of wood? What if there were fresh outbreaks of violence? How could the rabble be pacified?

To everyone's relief, as daylight lifted upon the ghastly scene in the park, and as the people assembled in thousands to gawk at the deliberate piecemeal dismantling of their famous old oak, not a voice nor a finger was lifted in protest. On the contrary, the people stood curiously silent, stunned like cattle, as though not quite awake. Perhaps initially all were wondering—half-expectantly, half-fearfully—whether the tree in its last moments might actually burst forth once again into speech. But when it became clear that no such event would occur, and that really this sacrosanct marvel of theirs was nothing more than a glorified stack of cordwood—then, at some indefinable moment, disillusionment modulated into outrage, and people of all different factions began rallying together and turning upon the tree as one single man to boisterously cheer its demise.

Suddenly the very air was swimming with a smell and a taint as of blood, as citizens, scientists, police, mystics, and politicians all began raising their fists and chanting aloud in unison:

"Yes, yes! Cut the thing down! Cut it down!"

Strangely, it was the first time in months that all parties seemed united in a common attitude toward the tree. And in the morning sun that day, as the great oak was reduced limb-by-limb to the level of the mob, violence turned inscrutably to brotherhood. For even before the sawdust had settled the townsfolk were talking amicably together, then drifting away and returning placidly to their homes and jobs; the tourists and vagrants and fanatics were dispersing; the last of the scientists were packing up their instruments; and Jessica's father and all his councilors were patting themselves on the backs and heaving enormous sighs of relief as peace and harmony were restored once again to their quiet, tree-lined streets.

Here, indeed, was a miraculous cure. And never again after that did any of them hear another word from the troublesome talking tree.

A year or so later, however, one Sunday morning the child Jessica happened to be out playing in those same woods at the edge of the park. And as she came across the familiar site of the felled oak tree, there was something new about it now that caught her eye: For today, growing straight up out of the center of the old dead stump, she noticed a fresh green shoot!

Immediately a rush of wonder swept through her, and drawing closer, Jessica knelt down in the soft earth and stared for a long, long time at the tiny trumpeting sprig of delicate foliage. And although it did not speak to her with audible words like that of the great talking oak she remembered so well, nevertheless this new young stalk was so straight and noble, and its crisp green color so lively, and the minuscule leaflets so fine and fresh and tender as they uncurled from their buds like little scrolls, that somehow Jessica heard once again the marvelous voice, and this time was left without a shadow of a doubt as to what it was that the infant tree was saying to her.

At least, that is what she always claimed forever afterwards.

The stories kids tell!

* * *

Moses saw that the bush burned with fire, but was not consumed ... And the voice of the Lord called to him from within the bush—"Moses! Moses! ... Take off your shoes, for the place where you are standing is holy ground."
Exodus 3:2ff.

How the Chipmunk Got His Stripes

IN THE DAYS OF THE GREAT FLOOD, when so much water covered the earth that even the peaks of all the highest mountains were submerged, the Spirit of the Lord brooded over the face of the deep, just as He had done in the very beginning.

Meanwhile old Noah, Captain of the S.S. Ark, was also busy brooding, lying in his hammock with hands clasped behind his head and staring at the pitch-smeared walls of his tiny stateroom. What good was it being saved, he was thinking, if only to be nailed up inside a big floating coffin with a pack of mangy fleabags? For although the rains had finally stopped falling, and the floodgates of the heavens and the springs of the deep had been shut, still for more than a hundred days the Ark drifted aimlessly, like a ghost ship, over the alien waves. And during this anxious time of waiting, the animals, quite naturally, had been growing more and more restless.

This very moment, in fact, Birds were flying in circles throughout the Ark, and scrapping. Cats caterwauled, and Jackals howled. The Camels had gotten progressively ornery (even more ornery than Camels generally got), and the Giraffes craned their necks to see what they could see, which was nothing. As for the Elephants, they had taken to pacing the decks, causing dangerous listing. And the Monkeys? Well, the Monkeys were simply impossible.

"My land!" groaned Noah—what a nervewracking voyage it had been!

Yet even more restless and vexatious than any of the other animals in this motley crew was the little Chipmunk named Jacob. He was a high-strung and claustrophobic enough creature as it was, without being cooped up for months on end with all creation inside a big overgrown egg made out of gopherwood.

Right from Day One Jacob Chipmunk had climbed the walls, making a total pest out of himself. If he wasn't sitting up insolently on his haunches on one of the highest beams, scolding and chattering away for hours on end in a voice like a rusty hinge, then he was racing up and down the narrow gangways, forever getting under foot or hoof.

Time and again Captain Noah had had to bawl him out.

"Hey, Mister Monk!" he would roar. "Why can't you settle down? In this Ark of mine there are many cabins—and one of them is especially made for Chipmunks! Why can't you go in there and stay put?"

But Jacob Chipmunk could not stay put. Either his legs or his mouth (or preferably both at once) had to be in motion. It was as if he were eating a steady diet of jumping beans.

"Jake Monk!" warned Captain Noah. "Either you settle down, or *I'll settle you down!*"

It wasn't that the Chipmunk didn't respect old Noah. And it certainly wasn't the case that he was trying on purpose to be a troublemaker. On the contrary, he did his level best to be a good and obedient creature. But somehow he just couldn't manage it. Not every minute of every day. And especially not under such confining circumstances. After all, he was a Chipmunk, not a Shipmunk! He desperately needed something to occupy him, to keep the old paws busy. Why wasn't there anything to DO on this big old tub? By the end of five months, he was hanging from the chandeliers.

Finally, with his teeth so on edge (literally) that he absolutely could not keep still for another solitary second, Jacob Chipmunk started thinking to himself, "Maybe if I just had something to chew on ..."

Yes, that was it! Something to chew on! Why hadn't he thought of it before? Of course, gopherwood was by no means his favorite. But as matters stood, it was all there was to be had.

Luckily, Jake possessed enough common sense not to try out his teeth on the hull of the boat. Instead, he chose a place high up in a corner near the top deck, where no one could see him. And there he set to work, gnawing and nibbling.

From that day on, the entire Ark began to heave a sigh of relief. For somehow, without anyone realizing quite why, things had grown a whole lot quieter all of a sudden. An animal could get a decent night's sleep for a change. And occasionally, one could even hear the waves lapping against the bow of the Ark. It was almost as though not just one Chipmunk, but a thousand had quit chattering.

Thus one day passed in relative peace, and then another, and another, until eventually Jacob Chipmunk had managed to chew his way right through the roof of the Ark, pitch and all. And so it happened that one Sunday morning a certain furry little brown head poked its way through into broad daylight, and suddenly found itself gazing out over more water than it had ever beheld in all its born days. There was water, water, everywhere, as far as two shiny black button eyes could see. Even the sky looked like water, Jake thought—if there *was* a sky, that is. For thick gray clouds were still draped overhead, and the horizon was nowhere to be found.

At this sight, the Chipmunk let out a long, slow whistle. And then, feeling for a moment as if he might be seasick, he went scampering across the topmost deck and hung his head over the railing. Yet even as he peered down over the side he caught sight of something which he had almost despaired of ever seeing again: *Dry Land!* Yes, directly beneath the Ark there was a small patch of dry land, the only bare ground to be seen in that whole wide watery realm. For the fact of the matter was, Jacob had been so preoccupied with the important business of gnawing his hole, that he hadn't even noticed that the big floating football had actually stopped floating and had finally come to rest.

Wasting no time, Jake Chipmunk skittered down the side of the Ark and planted his four tiny paws on the barren outcrop that was the peak of Mount Ararat, and kissed his Mother Earth. She was a little soggy, maybe—yet how solid and good she felt! Then, trying out his land legs, Jake did about three dozen laps around the hull of the Ark, first one way, then the other, and when that was finished he stretched himself up to his full height on two feet, tuckered and winded but nonetheless exhilarated. Shielding his eyes with one little paw like a sailor, he scanned out once more over the limitless expanse of gray, undulating floodwaters.

And that was when Jacob Chipmunk had his vision. Certainly no mystic by nature, nevertheless all in a flash he saw the Ark breaking open like a seed pod, and all the creatures spilling out of it and spreading once again throughout the whole land, filling the earth and multiplying.

It was a wonderful vision. Something to thrill the grandest of minds, let alone the fuzzy little acorn-brain of a Chipmunk. But there was one problem with it, and that was: How could the animals fill the earth, when the earth was all covered over with water? At present there was hardly room for a creature to set its foot, let alone to multiply. As for the pittance of dry land that was available, one Chipmunk alone had already used that up!

Jake scratched his noggan. Comparing his vision with the staggering reality of the infinite ocean before him, it didn't take a great genius to figure out that something here was going to have to change. And if something was going to have to change, then it only stood to reason that somebody was going to have to change it. Somebody would have to get off his duff and *do something*.

All at once, Jacob Chipmunk was converted into being not just a visionary, but a *missionary*—an animal with a mission! For here indeed was something to keep the old paws busy. Here was something to DO!

Immediately Jake flew into action, and as usual he did the first thing that popped into his mind, without wasting any time thinking about it. Racing down to the very edge of the lapping waves, he turned his backside toward them and gingerly dipped his fine bushy tail into the water. Oh, how cold it was! And how was a Chipmunk to navigate when his primary organ of balance was sopping wet? But for an animal with a mission, was any hardship too great? And so, like a streak, Jake raced back up to the top of the little rise on which the Ark was perched like a beached whale, and there he took his soaking wet tail in two paws and wrung it out until every last drop was gone.

This action produced the minutest of silver puddles on the surface of the water-logged ground. But already Jake was back at the shoreline, dipping his tail once more into the brimming flood. Again he dashed to the peak, paused there just long enough to squeeze out every drop of moisture, then sprinted back. So up and down he went, back and forth like a weaver's shuttle, like a one-animal bucket brigade, and all that was in his mind was the one single task at hand: to bail out the whole world!

Before long a rivulet had formed, trickling from the peak of the mountain right back down into the boundless bosom of the ocean, a distance of some few feet. On his way up the Chipmunk ran straight through the little stream, getting his paws and belly completely soaked in it, and on his way back down he raced its sliding, burbling quicksilver. He knew the stream was there, all right; he saw it out of the corner of his eye—and yet only as one may be aware, perhaps, that one's hair is turning gray. Somewhere in the back of his mind, in other words, Jake did have some faint inkling as to the inevitable fate of his little project. Still, what difference did it make? What, after all, could be done about it? No, the dim knowledge that he was working against indomitable forces of time and tide only spurred him on to work all the harder. For this was a Chipmunk with a mission! To be sure, it was a staggering task he had undertaken—but who else was going to do it? Who else but a visionary full-of-beans Chipmunk?

All of a sudden, however, right in the middle of this urgent mission—indeed, smack dab in the middle of one of these all-important shuttle-trips, and just at a point when Jacob had managed to blot up a particularly impressive tailful of water—just then, something happened to stop the Chipmunk cold in his tracks. As improbable as it may sound, something like an enormous hand reached down out of the blue and actually scooped him up on its broad, flat palm. And the next thing Jake knew, the hand was lifting him high, high up into the sky, like a highspeed elevator, all the way up to the very peak of the heavens.

"Hey! Put me down!" squealed Jake, though his heart was in his mouth. "Put me down! Put me down! Can't you see I'm busy!"

For now another vision, and this time a most exasperating one, was passing before the Chipmunk's eyes: For he was seeing all the water, all that precious water which he had so assiduously mopped up with his tired tail, now dribbling away again and being reabsorbed into the endless sea. Even if the worker were absent only a few minutes, he knew all the costly fruit of his diligent labors would go right down the drain (or, if you like, *not* go down the drain).

But just then, as if in answer to this very protest, Jake heard a voice speaking to him out of the clouds. And somehow he knew, instantly and beyond any doubt, that this was none other than the voice of the Almighty, his Lord and Creator.

"Jacob! Jacob!" called the voice. "What is it you are so busy at? What are you doing, my little Monk?"

Jake thought to himself: "Can't you see? Can't you see? I'm mopping up this fine mess You've made ..." (although of course he did not dare say such a thing out loud).

"But Jacob Chipmunk!" came the voice again. "Listen to Me: How can one tiny creature expect to mop up oceans and oceans of deep water with a single spindly tail? Do you really think you can perform such a great task all by yourself?"

There was something about hearing the voice of the Lord God Almighty which put a small Chipmunk to silence. Creeping then to the very tip of the shortest finger on the great hand, Jake peeked timidly over the edge. Oh—how high up they were! And what a tremendous amount of water there was down below! Even the big old Ark, that monstrous floating barn of Captain Noah's, appeared from this height to be barely the size of one of Jake's toenails.

"You see?" intoned the voice. "The task is beyond you, isn't it? It would be an easier thing just to turn yourself into a fish!"

This last comment was intended as a joke. But Jacob Chipmunk was not laughing. In fact, he was actually starting to cry. There was just something about being held in such a great hand, in the hand of one's own Creator, that touched the very heart of a Chipmunk. Even a petulant, hyperactive Chipmunk like this one.

"Now, watch Me," said the voice of the Lord. "Be silent, Jacob, and rest. And behold what I am going to do."

What happened next was something too astonishing, too wonderful, for words. Jake saw it happen, with his own two beady eyes, and yet those eyes were so filled with tears, and the thing he saw was so astounding, that afterwards he wondered whether he might possibly have dreamed it. And yet, what sort of dream could it be, from which one never again woke up?

For what happened was this: The Almighty heaved a great sigh. The Spirit of the Lord took a deep breath, a great, fathomless breath, and then He blew it out in one long, smooth stream of warm wind over the measureless gray desert of the flooded world. And at the mere touch of that breath, all the oceans of water became in an instant like a single drop of dew, then vanished like mist in the sun. It was as though a heavy lace veil covering the face of the earth had all at once been whisked away. Suddenly there was green and brown again, and there were tall mountains and broad plains, and rolling hills and mighty forests and meadows filled with flowers. And there were oceans too—only now the oceans were in their places—and there were waterfalls and rushing rivers and shining lakes held as though in the hollow of a hand.

And finally, as the warm wind of the Almighty's breath subsided, one last marvel occurred like a grand finale: *The sun came out!* Instantly the great blue-and-green globe was drenched with immaculate, dancing light! Then, taking some of the light and bending it delicately between thumb and forefinger, the hand of the Lord Creator fashioned a brightly-colored archway in mid-air. And at that point, just as in the Chipmunk's vision, Noah's Ark indeed cracked wide open like the shell of an Easter egg, and all the creatures came pouring out of it and paraded beneath the magnificent archway as though in triumphal procession—crawling, leaping, prancing, flying, and swarming over the whole earth, covering it with something that was even more beautiful than light: *Life.*

"Do you see, my little Chipmunk?" whispered the voice of the Lord. "Do you see what I can do?"

With these words, the great hand gently lowered Jacob Chipmunk down onto the dry land, placing him on a soft bed of sweet-smelling needles and bits of cone, deep within a forest of cool dark cedars where the sunlight came lancing in buttery shafts through the green-gold lattice of branches. A place of the heart's desire.

Just before the hand was withdrawn, however, the tips of the fingers brushed once, lightly, along Jacob's head and back, leaving a most profound and mysterious impression upon the little Chipmunk. For somehow it seemed, this mystic stroke, to be a combination of two things, two things impossibly different: In one way, it was like the long-ago memory of his own mother's tongue, licking him; but also it was like the claws of a great bird of prey raking through his flesh.

The pain, however, was only for a moment, while the delicious sensation of the tenderest of caresses remained forever. And along with it came four beautiful white stripes, embedded in the Chipmunk's fur, running the length of his body and set like a crown on the top of his head: the sign of being stroked by the Almighty's love.

After that, the hand of the Lord released him. And although he went scampering off immediately to explore his new forest and to track down all his friends and relatives, there was now a new thoughtfulness that marked all his activity. For ever afterwards Jacob Chipmunk took his way a bit more slowly, and wisely, through the world.

How the Chipmunk Got His Stripes

* ✻ *

I am the Lord...Who says to the watery deep, "Be dry!"
   Isaiah 44:27

Scarecrow

We are the hollow men
We are the stuffed men
Leaning together
Headpiece filled with straw. Alas!
T.S. Eliot

HERE IN STRAWVILLE things keep pretty quiet, mostly. Everybody minds his own business, and us straw folks get along okay. But we had ourselves a little fracas not so long ago. And seein's how you's a stranger here and all, mister, I don't mind fillin' you in on it.

Wellsir, seems this young feller—oddball sort—gets it into his fool head one day he's a-gonna change the farmin' system round here. Starts pushin' his newfangled ideers, see. Now, every man's got a right to his own opinions. But this little whippersnapper seemed to think the whole bloomin' world ought to run his way. And when you start tryin' to shove stuff down people's throats—well, folks don't take none too kindly to that. 'Specially seein's how this feller never actually run a farm himself. All he ever done, see, was work on his daddy's place. Said as much himself. 'Twas his daddy done run the whole show.

But like I say, this kid had a oddball streak. Different sorta guy. Weren't right in the head, I guess. 'Course, in the beginnin' none of us had any notion how downright contrary he really was. After all, everybody's a character, one way or t'other, and this one done growed up right hereabouts. Just to look at him, he was same as anybody else: big straw hat on his straw head, shiny black button eyes, straw stickin' out his sleeves and cuffs, hayseed in his ears. Just your regular redneck strawboy. So for a long time, see, he done fit right in.

But then he up and starts spoutin' all this fancy radical stuff. All them highfalutin' ideers about weed control and irrigation, for instance, and some new kinda purebred seed and so on. Why, he even tries to tell us old hands how to plough a straight furrow! Some nerve, I tell you. Thinks he's got everythin' all figgered out, he does. And since he's such a smooth talker and all, he gets a lotta the fellers eatin' right outa his hand.

Well, ain't nothin' wrong with that. There's always been fools, and always will be. And fools need other fools to get fooled by.

But it's when he starts talkin' crows—that's when things really begin heatin' up. 'Cause crows, you ought to know, is a mighty touchy subject round Strawville here. You don't just go shootin' off your mouth about crows, if you know what's good for you. But not havin' growed up round these here parts, mister, it may be you ain't catchin' my meanin' real clear. So let me spell it out for you plain-like:

The crows hereabouts, they ain't no ordinary birds—nossir! For one thing, they's blacker than the blackest crow—or raven—you ever done seen. Black as the ace of spades at night. And big, too. Big as eagles, some of 'em. And meaner than a turkey vulture. Why, they've got claws and fangs on 'em like the tines of a pitchfork—and that ain't stretchin' it much. You got to see one of these here critters to believe it.

Fall is when they's worst. Right when the corn's come up high and green and thick and pretty, and the tassles gleam golden, and the cobs inside is sweet and fat and creamy yeller. That's when them galldarned crows bands together, and they sits in the woods at sunrise and makes the big trees shudder and rock with their strawcurdlin' croaks. They's just like a cycle gang itchy for action, or like a whole black-cassocked congregation of slope-shouldered hell-breathin' preachers. And when they comes a-spewin' out over the valley like some kinda black vomit, darkenin' the sky at noon and settlin' down over the choicest fields and all day long a-fillin' and a-stuffin' their black holler bellies till they's bloated as cows—wellsir, I tell you the truth: Time they get done with a body's crop, it ain't worth a handful of chicken crap.

She's a heartbreaker, for sure. Standin' by and watchin' a beauty of a cornfield gettin' picked clean as bone, whole year's work up in smoke. Mighty hard to take, she is. Oh, there's the odd field gets left, and in a bad year all us farmers pull together pretty good and pool what we got. So there's usually enough to put seed in the ground for next year, and try again. But believe me, mister, there ain't never a whole slew of a lot to go round, nossir. Us straw people is poor folks—and I mean poor. Long's anybody can remember, them deuced crows been eatin' us outa house and home.

And there ain't a blasted thing you can do about it. Year in, year out, them critters always come. 'Nuff to wear a guy down to a frazzle, she is. But when you been round here as long as I been, and you seen a thing or two, you learn just to shut up and take her. You learn that it ain't so bad livin' with a few growls down inside your tummy. 'Cause one thing's for sure: There don't nobody go messin' with them crows, nossir. And that's all there is to it.

'Cause I'll tell you why. A strawman goes near one of them crows, and he gets himself torn to shreds. Simple as that. Fact is, there ain't nothin' a mean old crow likes better than gettin' his long filthy claws into a nice straw-packed head or chest and a-rippin' and a-peckin' her to bits. Mister, they just *loves* that human straw, and in two shakes of a stick there ain't nothin' left of a feller but a pile of old rags. Don't matter who you are, fancy-dress city slicker or no-good bum, them crows cuts everybody right down to the same size. Why, now and again—just to keep folks honest, I guess—you hear tell of a big crow come swoopin' down and snatchin' up some little child, clean off the ground, and carryin' 'em off. Sure, she's a ugly business. Ain't nice even to whisper such things. But that there's the kinda critters we's dealin' with.

'Course, every once in a while a buncha young daredevils get theirselves all tanked up in the bar and starts talkin' rowdy about the terrible crow problem. And maybe a few of 'em even go troopin' on out into some field wavin' broken bottles and broomsticks, hopin' to scare the varmints off or somethin'. But it ain't no use. Don't nobody like that never survive to tell the tale. 'Cause when it come right down to the crunch, see, us strawmen just ain't no match for them big black buzzards.

But I'll fill you in on somethin' else: With these here crows, there's one thing works pretty good. One, and one only. And it's a funny thing, but round here she's supposed to be a big secret, all hush-hush and so on. Not that the whole county don't know about it. But she's the kinda secret, see, that everybody's in on, but don't nobody never talk about. Somethin' you might call *off limits* to polite conversation. I only mention it, mister, seein's you's a stranger here and all. Just so's you won't go stickin' your foot into your big trap by mistake. So listen:

Whenever any of us strawfolks dies—which is somethin' happens fairly regular, believe me—we got ourselves a little custom that's been round long's anybody remembers. What we do, see, is instead of buryin' the dead body, we takes her out into one of the fields and ties her up to a stake. And that there's what folks round here refers to as a *scarecrow*, see. 'Course, she ain't your regular garden variety scarecrow. 'Cause like I been sayin', we all know there ain't nothin' gonna scare away them sorta crows—nossir! 'Stead, whenever we stakes up these here strawcorpses out in the fields, what happens is that the mangy critters come right along and kinda clean them bodies up for us. Polish 'em off, see. Or to put it real plain-like: what they does is they pecks and pecks away at the old shell, till there ain't nothin' left. 'Cause if there's one thing them crows likes better, it seems, than a live strawman, it's a dead 'un.

Now I can appreciate how all this maybe sounds a mite grisly to you, mister, bein' an outsider. But believe me, this little method we got works real nice. The whole job gets done in the dead of night, so's nobody has to watch, and in the mornin' all's left of the scarecrow is a few rags and a empty stake. No fuss, see, no muss, and no undertaker to worry about.

Scarecrow

But the real beauty part is what comes next: 'Cause wherever them crows done et up a corpse in a cornfield, after that them varmints stays clean away from that there crop. Clean away! I tell you, she's a regular miracle. Don't matter how big and juicy them cobs get, ain't no crow gonna blacken that there field where a scarecrow's been et. Works just like a charm, like a magic spell over the land. Leastwise—till next year. Then, as only stands to reason, we got to start all over again from scratch.

But strange critters they is, them crows. Some folks say, it ain't really corn they's after at all. Seems like the one thing somehow satisfies 'em is *death*. Yessir, a dead body's just like candy to 'em.

Why, there's even the odd farmer who'll *kill* another strawman, just to save his field. It ain't common, but I heard tell of it. And then, the poor weaklin' strawfolk, and them that go bad, and the sick 'uns, they don't none of 'em last too long round here. Just can't afford to keep 'em, see. Not when there's healthy mouths to feed.

So here in Strawville, we got our own ways of dealin' with the crow problem. Mite crude, maybe, but she sure does the trick. This here's how we always done her, and this here's how we always *will* do her. 'Cause when you get right down to it, with crows there just ain't nothin' else works.

Maybe you can appreciate now why crows is such a awful delicate subject round here, and why this young upstart feller with his newfangled ideers started gettin' a few folks a mite riled. Now, if he'd a-stuck to pushin' his jimdandy seed and his straight furrows, see, he mighta done all right and been left alone. But the one big thing he kept harpin' on, more and more as time went on, was this:

We shouldn't oughta be givin' the dead bodies to the crows, says he. *Scarecrows is no good*, says he. *She's a infernal practice, and she's gotta go.*

"So what we gonna do?" folks asks him. "How we gonna eat? Without them corpse fields, there ain't nothin' left for us."

Wellsir, this feller kinda gets up on his high horse and he says to us all:

The only reason you's afeerd of them crows is 'cause you's all made outa straw in your innards. What you gotta do is to get aholt of some real manflesh—that's what he called her—*and when you done that, then you can go out into them fields*, says he, *and fight off them crows yourselves.*

"With our bare hands?!" everybody yelps. "You gotta be outa your mind! Them critters'd rip us all to shreds!"

Not if you got some real manflesh in your bellies, says he.

And then all the strawfolks wants to know: "So where we gonna get this here *manflesh* stuff you're talkin' about?"

And you know what this feller does then? He smiles real mystery-like, and he points straight at himself. Done plunks a straw thumb smack dab in the middle of his own straw chest, and declares:

Eat me. You gotta eat me. This here body of mine might look like plain old straw to you, but it ain't. Inside, it's meat. Real meat. And you gotta eat it. Eat this meat, says he, *and them crows won't give you no more nevermind. And you won't never have no more growlin' bellies nevermore.*

Wellsir, a line of nonsense like that don't go over none too well with the strawfolks. Why, it just ain't right to go danglin' pie-in-the-sky in front of hungry people. And just the tone of voice he used in talkin' about our beautiful golden strawbodies, makin' them out to be cheaper than dirt, and then tryin' to stir us all up to go out and get ourselves kilt grapplin' with crows with our bare knuckles and all—mister, I tell you, it just weren't much to our likin', to say the least. And as for this here other claptrap, about eatin' some kinda *flesh*—well, he made it sound like he wanted us all to turn into crows ourselves and start gobblin' each other up! If you ask me, that there's crazy talk. Guy like that just ain't right in the head, nossir.

And whenever a strawman goes right round the bend like that, what's a decent bunch of folks supposed to do? Like I says, there's too many healthy mouths to feed, without stuffin' the sick 'uns too. So when you got some holy terror on your hands, it don't take long before the tide turns agin him, and folks starts plottin' how to give him the old heave-ho and feed him to the crows. Now, I admit, in this case things maybe got a trifle outa hand. Can't say myself I exactly approve of the way she all was handled, I mean with the trial and all. And 'specially stringin' him up in broad daylight the way they done. But it seems like there was a few rowdies just couldn't wait to get their hands on him. And who knows, maybe they was right. Finish him off fast, see, 'fore he gets to smoothtalkin' his way out of it.

Anyway, early one mornin—and a fine, sunshiny mornin' it were too—a bunch of these here rowdies lays aholt on him, right there on his daddy's spread, and drags him out into a cornfield. "You wanna fight crows," they tells him, "you can darn well fight crows." And so they ties him up to a stake out there under God's own sky—still alive and breathin', see. A gruesome joke, you might say, but that's what they done. And then, 'stead of just stealin' away all dignity-like and leavin' the wretch to himself, a few of us fellers made the mistake of sittin' in our trucks at the edge of the field, just to watch what'd happen.

Yeah, I have to admit, I was there too. Seen her all for myself, though I didn't have no part of her. I mean, she all happened so fast, and if anybody's to blame for the way things turned a bit screwy there and ran clean off the rails, I figger it was the feller himself, with all his holier-than-thou ideers. But one thing's for sure: I won't never forget that moment when them crows comes a-swoopin' down outa the hills like a pack of hungry wolves, or like a dark ol' thunderhead, and goes a-swarmin' like ants all over that strung-up body. For a while there you couldn't see a blamin' thing 'cept for a cloud of pitch black feathers chock fulla yeller beaks and claws, and all nippin' and tearin' away to beat the band. But then, sudden like, midst all that ruckus, I looks and I sees somethin' that makes me sit up real straight, and rub my eyes, and look again. And then I turns to the wife and I says, "Hey! Looky there! You see what I see?" And sure enough, she done see it same as me. 'Cause right there in plain daylight, I swear, just like somethin' in a dream, them crows starts a-turnin' bright red and a-droppin' like flies!

I tell you, I didn't know whether to laugh, cry, lean on the horn, or what. I mean, far as anybody round here was concerned, them varmints was sheer indestructible. Weren't no way at all to get at 'em, let alone make 'em *bleed*. Fact is, none of us'd ever even seen crowsblood before. Yet there she was, big gobs of scarlet shinier than a bird's eyeballs, and there was them crows just a-layin' like winos all over the ground and a-leakin' away like sieves.

Leastwise, that's the way we had her figgered at first. But then we finds out that what's really goin' on is somethin' even weirder than that—'cause as more and more of them crows keeps fallin' away and hittin' the dust, suddenly we sees, lookin' real close, that it ain't the critters what's spillin' out that red muck at all. Nossir—it's the young feller at the stake!

Man alive, that there done give us a mighty queer feelin', just seein' that strawbody of his all torn and hangin' in shreds and, well, *bleedin'*. 'Cause listen here, mister: for crows to have blood is one thing. But *mansblood*—that's an entire different story. Like somethin' *inhuman* if you ask me. 'Nuff to make the old innards crawl, the way that juice kept a-pourin' out from inside him, pourin' like red rain right out of his wounds—almost like you could see his bare heart exposed and pumpin' the stuff out. And not only that, but the more the blood came, the more them crows came too, just like they was gettin' sucked or pulled in by a big magnet. What I mean is, they starts appearin' outa nowhere, clear outa the next county and beyond, great flocks and clouds of 'em swarmin' from one horizon to the other, till in no time there ain't nothin' but one continuous river of inky black a-plungin' down towards that one man at the stake.

Wellsir, once I seen that, I didn't stick around none too long. Would you, mister? I mean, the whole sky black as night? And the earth itself shakin' with thunder from millions of wings? And all that glitterin' crimson gore gushin' out over the ground? I tell you, it was near enough to make a feller sick at his guts.

So I does what any decent citizen woulda done: I clears outa there real fast, and I drops the little woman off at home and then goes out to the café for bacon and eggs and coffee with the boys, same as always, and we don't none of us say one deuced word about none of these here goin's-on. She's all just business as usual, see, just like nothin' at all's ever happened. 'Cause believe me, mister, life is short, and there's crops to plant and machinery to fix and fence to mend and mouths to feed, and so on and so forth, and there just ain't no blessed time for no crazy claptrap.

I mean, what's it to me if I seen a buncha crows that day gettin' themselves slaughtered left and right, and a-layin' in piles on the field all round that feller's feet, with their bodies all twisted and busted up and their feathers crudded and sticky-red—what's it to me, I say? 'Cause if that's what it takes to kill them buggers off, then you can count me out. I wash my hands of it. And I'll tell you somethin' else, mister: In spite of what happened that day, there's more of them blasted crows round here now than there ever was. Yessir, it's a fact. So just like I say, there ain't no way to get rid of 'em. Kill off one, and seven more rushes in to take its place.

Sure, I know, there's all kinds of talk goin' round. People tellin' stories about this and that happenin', and yakkin' away about this feller and all the great things he done. And then there's folks like you streamin' in from all across the country just to see what the big fuss is about and all. But you're wastin' your time, if you ask me. Even this here story about the cornfield where the feller died: I don't pay her no heed no more. Wouldn't go near her with a ten-foot pole. Oh yeah, maybe what you heard is true, the way three days after the lynchin' the corn there starts a-sproutin' away like crazy, shootin' up thick and green and high as the sky, and overnight she produces the biggest bumper crop anybody round here's ever seen, and not only that, but them cobs is the sweetest, lushest grub you'll ever taste this side of heaven.

Oh yeah, I know all about it. Can't tell me nothin' new. Even went myself to some of these here big corn feeds they hold for the tourists, just to have a lookysee. But mister, I tell you for a fact, I never actually tasted none of that corn myself. Never let her pass my lips, never even sniffed her. And most of us local folks, we's all the same. We wouldn't touch that stuff for no love nor money. 'Cause I'll tell you why: We *knowed* that feller. We knowed him personal. Growed right up with him, we did. And all of us knowed firsthand, see, how crazy in the head he was. Yessir, we knowed everything there was to know about him, just like we knows our own selves.

And we also knows bloomin' well what it is what made that there cornfield grow so terrible good. Yessir, we knows what done her alright: 'Twas that there blood. That's what done her. 'Twas all that spilt blood soakin' down through the dirt and then runnin' all through that crop like wildfire.

So that there's the whole story, mister, beginnin' to end, and now she's up to you. You want to go pourin' blood like manure all over your crops, then you go right on ahead. But you can count me out, that's for sure. 'Cause if you ask me, the whole flamin' business is spookier than hell.

Yessir, she's spookier than hell.

* * *

I tell you the truth, unless you eat the flesh of the Son of Man, and drink His blood, you have no life in you.
John 6:53

What Really Happened at Multnomah Falls

I

On the Columbia River in Oregon, not far from the city of Portland, there is a beautiful waterfall that looks like a single long braid of silver hair. Every waterfall celebrates that mysterious capacity of water to burst suddenly into bolts of white crinoline, then to draw together again in dark pools, silent and reflective, as though nothing had ever happened. But at Multnomah Falls, an even deeper mystery is celebrated.

For when the wind blows upon the narrow, elegant column of this falls, as a man might press his hand against a woman's waist, the water bends, sways like a snake in a basket, and then blurs out over the rockface in shifting clouds of spray. And at one point, as the gossamer strands go drifting across the cliff, a face appears, hidden in the rock wall—the profile of a figure veiled behind the mist. But as soon as the breeze releases its hold again, immediately the veil falls away and the face disappears, fading back into blank rock.

Whose face is this, revealed by a veil? It's a fleeting vision, appearing only for a moment at that mystical juncture in which water, wind, and rock see eye to eye, united in a certain revelatory caprice. And because it is the face of a moment only, it is also somehow the face of eternity—as when worlds part, and reality for an instant surrenders its secret.

Whose face is this?

Local legend has it that this is the face of Multnomah, an Indian princess of the Walamet people. It seems that one spring the Walamets had been struck by a terrible plague. Many lay dying, and countless prayers and religious rituals had been offered up, yet all to no avail. Finally a medicine man named Wah-si-ak-li had come before the band council quoting an ancient prophecy, which stated that a time was coming when the ire of the Great Spirit was destined to break out against the Walamets, and they would be totally annihilated. Their one hope of salvation, declared Wah-si-ak-li, would be the blood sacrifice of a royal maiden, pure and innocent, who at a certain spot along the Big River must throw herself down from the topmost point of the cliff onto the rocks below.

Now Multnomah was the daughter of Kalipuya, the Chief of the Walamets. She was a spotless virgin, as beautiful as the dawn, and when the shaman had given his counsel, all eyes turned naturally toward this royal maiden, and all thoughts fell upon her with a weight heavier than that of all the water in the Big River plunging down on top of her at once. She might as well have been stoned to death on the spot.

Kalipuya, however, gazing in pain upon this only daughter of his, gave Wah-si-ak-li this noble and unforgettable reply:

"Better would it be by far for every man, woman, and child in our tribe to die of this sickness, than that our survival should be purchased in such a barbaric manner."

As Chief, Kalipuya had the final word. And so for the moment that was the end of the matter.

Yet the plague continued unabated, until even the strongest of the people began to succumb to it like eagles clipped of their wings. Indeed, eventually the sickness reached Klaat-tu, the brave young warrior who was betrothed to Multnomah. And when the beautiful maiden saw the plague fever burning upon the face of her lover, immediately she knew what she had to do. Going to her father, she first asked him, then begged him again and again with tears, to allow her to carry out the dreadful sacrifice prescribed by Wah-si-ak-li.

At length the old Chief, his heart crushed by the looming specter of the extinction of his people, relented. What else was to be done? How could mere men stand against the wrath of spirits? And who could say whether Multnomah herself might not be the next to fall sick?

At first light the next morning, therefore, Multnomah made her way alone to the top of the cliff, climbing all the way up to the precise point from which the rocks poured forth the tall silver snake of a waterfall, the very falls that one day would bear her own name. This was the spot designated by the medicine man, and as the frightened young maiden stood there in the palm of fate, rather than staring down at the rocks below she tried to focus her gaze upon the grand vista of the Big River as it stretched out magnificently to east and to west. Yet no matter where she looked, it was still a dizzying, sickening height. And a terrible thought began to creep over her, as eerily she realized that the thing she feared most was not the moment when her frail body would be crushed against the rocks. No. What she really was afraid of was falling forever.

At the same time, strangely, it seemed to Multnomah that never in all her life had the world looked more beautiful to her than it did in that moment. The dawn air was exquisitely pure, the pale spring sky tinged ever so faintly with rose, just like a petal or a baby's cheek. No breeze ruffled the hair of the falls this morning. The narrow roaring column fell straight down into the gorge, the water white as a wedding veil.

Meanwhile, back in the village, hundreds of her people waited for the moment when one of their own, by taking a single step, would send herself as a gift from one world into the next, a gift that was destined to deliver the entire Walamet nation from death.

That fateful moment had come. Multnomah took the step, gave the dread gift. She leaped into the waiting arms of the morning ...

II

That, at least, is how the legend goes.

Multnomah leaped, and like a part of the waterfall itself her perfect young body went sailing over the cliff, her long hair streaming. If she cried out then or uttered any word at all, the sound of it was lost in the rush and boil of her own Multnomah Falls as it shouted *hosanna!* into the gorge below.

Later that morning, it was a solemn band of men who found the maiden's remains splayed upon the rocks, and who buried her there beside the Big River. And yes—even before they got back to the village that day, the miracle had happened, and that very hour the scourge of the plague had been lifted from their midst. People who had lain sick, right at death's door, got up out of their beds literally running and dancing! And oh! what great celebration there was then among the Walamets! What laughing, and weeping, and feasting, and rejoicing! For the Great Spirit had honored their sacrifice. The Great Spirit had heard their cry.

And so it is that today, whenever the wind brushes the falls and smears its spray over the cliff, the face of the princess Multnomah may be seen, emblazoned in the rock, crowned with mist. There for a moment—then gone. It is the face of peace with the Great Spirit.

At least, that is what the legend says ...

III

But the truth of the story, thank goodness, runs differently. For what really happened at Multnomah Falls, that rosy-cheeked dawn so long ago, was this:

The night before she was to die, it so happened that the royal maiden had a dream. In that dream she saw herself standing at the head of the falls and preparing her heart for the moment of sacrifice, when all at once, from somewhere behind and above her, she heard a voice, apparently coming out of the treetops.

"Multnomah!" whispered the voice, soft but urgent, almost like the wind. "What are you doing here?"

Craning her neck, Multnomah thought she could just make out the form of a man up there, high in the very top of one of the fir trees. Or was it only that the pattern of branches, in the faint dawn light, resembled a man's shape?

Impelled by the voice, and by the mystery, she went over to the base of the tree and began climbing up it, limb by limb. And the closer she drew to the top, the more real the man became. Unaccountably, he appeared to be caught in the branches, impaled somehow upon them, and clearly he was in anguish. But oh—how wonderfully handsome he was! How noble of visage and how tender-eyed! Who could this be, pondered the maiden: a man more fair and more entrancing, even, than her own beloved Klaat-tu?

At this point in her dream, just as Multnomah reached the top of the tree, she chanced to look down. And as she did so, the sight that met her eyes pierced her with a sudden terror. For when her feet had been firmly planted on the ground, the top of the falls had appeared high—and yet how much higher she was now! Indeed, it seemed that the vista spread out below her now was not that of a single valley but of the whole wide world. And if prior to this the valley of the Big River had appeared to her (through the trick of her own nearness to death) especially and poignantly beautiful, now what she saw was a world veined and flowing not with rivers of shining water, but rather with raging torrents of blood and pus and vomit that ate like acid into the bedrock of the earth itself, tearing it away like so much rotting flesh.

It was a bone-chilling vision, horrific and dissolving. For the princess Multnomah saw with more clarity, perhaps, than an ordinary human mind could bear, that it was not merely her own people who were dying of disease. No, it was the whole world. It was life itself that was sick unto death. Where before she had seen the plague burnt into the face of her lover, now she saw it coiled like a viper within the very heart of the earth itself, and in her own heart as well.

At that point, therefore, in mortal fear the maiden turned to the man in the tree and in desperation threw her arms around him, clinging to him for dear life—indeed, for much more than life—yet only to find, to the staggering enlargement of her horror, that the man was dead! Stiff, cold, stone cold, dead. She was hugging a corpse ...

Right there the dream had broken off. With a shudder Multnomah awakened, bathed in sweat, white with trembling, and quickly she rose from her bed. Already the stars were fading from the sky as she took her way along the stony path that led to the top of the cliff above the Big River, up to the head of the snake-thin falls whose foaming waters poured hoar-colored, shroud-colored from the cave of the dawn. And there she stood, chilled, alone, empty, drained now of every thought and every passion. No shred of faith nor of hope was hers now, no scrap of illusion that the act she was about to carry out had anything at all to do with courage or nobility or goodness or love. No, the dream had robbed her of all that, leaving her only with a numbing sense of the utter futility of anything she might do, the odious vanity of all things human. No more could she believe in this sacrifice. No more could she believe in any sacrifice, nor in any religious act. All was sham, all was meaninglessness. Everything, in the end, turned to death in one's hands, everything stiffened to a stone cold corpse.

Thus the real Multnomah, as it turns out, was a very different person from the Multnomah of legend. And yet it was this Multnomah, and no other, who now prepared to leap to her death into the empty arms of the morning, and it was this Multnomah who would now perform her act not out of love for her dear Klaat-tu, nor out of heroic devotion to her people, but simply because there was no longer any reason for her to go on living. No sacrifice this was— but suicide.

Yet how could it be, even in the midst of such bleak and oppressive thoughts, that the world in that moment still looked to this young woman more achingly beautiful than she had ever seen it before? The sky, as pure and as delicate as a baby's skin, was so close it seemed to brush against her, almost to breathe, and the Big River was not blood and offal now, but liquid light, and in the gathering dawn the leaping falls shone white as a wedding veil.

Just at that point, exactly as in her dream, Multnomah heard a voice behind her. And looking around she saw a man stepping out from the shadows of the forest.

"Multnomah!" whispered the man, his voice softly strong like a lover's hand upon her waist. "What are you doing here?"

At once she knew that this indeed was the same figure she had dreamed of, the very one whose corpse had been impaled upon the tree. Yet now that corpse had walked right up to her and was standing at her side—alive! And much more than alive—how ravishingly lovely he was! Lovelier than the whole earth in its mantle of dawn. Fairer than the moon and all the stars.

"Multnomah!" he whispered again, like the wind, like rushing water. "What are you doing here?"

"I came to die ..." she stammered, breaking into sobs, "... to die for my people ... a sacrifice ..."

She felt somehow as though she were dead already: dead inside.

"Dear child, little princess," spoke the stranger, standing beside her even taller than the waterfall, yet still at her own level and gazing directly, tenderly into her eyes. "Do you not understand? Do you not know, in your heart, that your death will mean nothing, will add nothing? For the price of this plague is far greater than you can pay. Had you a million lives to lay down, still your sacrifice would not avail. Why, even the one life you have is not your own."

What Really Happened at Multnomah Falls

Multnomah stared. The man's eyes were like suns.

"But know this," he went on: "The sacrifice for your people has already been provided. The price has already been paid."

He spread wide his arms, as though to embrace her.

"It is true!" he declared. "It is for the Great Spirit Himself to provide the sacrifice; it is for you to provide faith—nothing more. All that remains is for you to add your own blessing to what has already been done. Only believe, only trust: for that is all you can do, and it is what you were made for. Have faith— have faith in me! Then you and your people will be saved."

With these words the man who was taller than the morning and who yet looked straight into the eyes, this man himself took that dread step which, by rights, ought to have been Multnomah's. For like a rainbow of mist, he slipped suddenly into the moving waterfall and vanished over the edge of the cliff—an act which took all of Multnomah's breath away and brought her heart right up into her mouth, and at the same time set her soul to singing. For it was almost as though, for the first time in her life, she had just seen the setting of the sun! True, the sun was gone now—but who could be sad for long with such magnificent colors spilling into the sky?

Therefore swift as an arrow and happy as a lark— oh, gloriously happy!—back she flew to her people then, back down the narrow stony path and into the valley, bursting with this new message that the mountain had spoken to her, skipping with the joy of it, her very blood laughing, her feet shod with the springing gladness of good news.

And when she arrived amongst her people, how was this jubilant messenger, this brand new daughter of the morning, received in her home village, her village of death? How was she welcomed in that place where every man, woman, and child had moldering death in their eyes, where even the healthy were filled up to the eyeballs with death merely from looking at death all day long? How did these walking dead greet their joyous princess, their living and lovely Multnomah who now bubbled around them as though somehow, up there on the cliff, she herself had been transformed into a waterfall?

"My sacrifice was not needed!" she proclaimed. "Someone died in my place! The Great Spirit Himself took the form of a man, and He died for me! It is not to be fathomed, it is only to be believed. Believe, believe, and you too will be saved!"

But the men and the women who had glittering death in their eyes did not believe. Instead, gathering around this mystery of joy and new life, they glared holes in it, pinned it to the ground with their stares, and believed not a word. And Wah-si-ak-li the medicine man was there too, hooded, joyless, glaring like a hawk.

"You lie!" he hissed. "You go to cliff, you cast eyes down—but body will not follow. Spirit say yes, but flesh say no. For your heart is woman's heart, coward's heart of water, not blood. And now you try to deceive, now you make up foolish story. Do we not die enough already, Multnomah, that today you must add your lies to our plague?"

At this, even the Chief Kalipuya, standing at a distance, hung his head in shame for his daughter. For what crime was more heinous than the telling of lies to the dying?

There followed a moment of dense silence, stiff with horror. And then in the people there welled up rage. All the pain and the grief and the hardness that was in them came out, and as one person they rushed upon the princess Multnomah and seized her and bound her like a buffalo calf with ropes. Then bearing her body rigid upon their shoulders as though already it were a corpse, they swarmed with a single-blooded instinct toward the path that led up to the cliff. And having reached the brow, the crown of the towering rock where the falls gushed forth like an open artery, there they spoke no prayer, wove no charm, performed no ritual, but rather mindlessly as beasts, savagely as children, they hurled the maiden's body into the chasm below.

No sacrifice was this—nor suicide—but plain murder.

And then they whooped. And stomped. And danced and danced, flinging their way back down the cliff and on into the village, beating drums and whirling and clapping and shouting and singing—

not for joy, to be sure, nor for any good reason at all. But merely to drown out death. Merely to cover over the terrible secret which their hearts knew so well, but which all the energy of their lives was expended in denying: the secret that there truly was no meaning to life.

IV

And yes: In a mystery of grace, death *was* drowned out that day. For that very hour the plague was lifted, and the sick ones literally rose from their beds and joined in the dance. For is God not merciful? And is not His mercy an unreasonable mercy, an irreverent mercy, as free and inscrutable as the wind? Does He not do whatever He pleases?

So yes: The Walamets were saved from extinction, and for a little while, at least, there was indeed true joy in their village once again, and true reason for dancing. Even the grim old heart of Wah-si-ak-li was, for a time, as glad as a boy's.

And yes: Even today the memorial of the miracle can still be seen. For there, etched into the very cliff beside Multnomah Falls, is the face. And when the smooth strong wind rests a hand upon the slender waist of the water and invites it to dance, and the skirts of the falls go swirling out and spread their spindrifting crinoline over the sheer gray rock—then the hardness of the rock, for a moment, seems to melt away, to roll away like mist in the sun until suddenly the wonderful face softly, magically appears, a regal face cameoed in spray, limned with diamonds.

And yes: Most who see this say it is the face of the Indian princess Multnomah. So they tell and re-tell the story of a young maiden's courage and purity and faith, and of the ultimate sacrifice she paid for the sake of the one she loved, and for her people: all of which is written about there on the memorial plaque erected by the white man's historical society.

And yet, some see another face in this cliff. Some see, that is, the face of Another—and not in the cliff only, but also in the falls itself, and in the forest, and in the valley of the Big River, and even in the invisible wind. For this is a face that is everywhere. And the story that is told of this other face, and of the man in the tree who by His death saved the world and brought an end to death everlastingly—this story, while perhaps not so pretty a tale as the legend of Multnomah, is the true story, and in the end a better story by far.

* * *

They built high places for Baal in the Valley of Ben Hinnom to sacrifice their sons and daughters to Molech—something I did not command, nor did it enter my mind.
    Jeremiah 32:35

The Garden of the Beatitudes

EVERYONE KNOWS the story of Gregor Mendel, the Father of Genetics. Everyone knows about his quaint experiments with sweet peas which, like the splitting of the atom, turned out to be seminal to the flowering of the modern age in all its peculiar beauty and terror. Everyone knows this story from having studied it religiously in school, almost as though it were a contemporary version of the Garden of Eden tale.

Not everyone knows, however, that the renowned Austrian monk had a younger brother named Johann, who also possessed a genius for botany, and who also engaged in genetic experimentation. Johann too became a monk at a young age (though he entered a different order from his brother), and for the next fifty years he devoted his energies to the patient crossbreeding of common plants. Nevertheless, while Johann did arrive at some interesting results, it must be admitted that by its very nature his work did not attract celebrity. On the contrary, it seemed to earn him only the scorn and ridicule of his colleagues at the Abbey of the Beatitudes.

One of Johann Mendel's earliest projects, for example, was the breeding of a variety of rose whose flower was perfectly transparent, like glass. Indeed, so colorless were the petals that they barely could be seen, and for this reason Johann's fellow monks made great sport of the curious new plant.

"What is the point of cultivating invisible flowers?" they laughed. But to Johann himself, this particular hybrid always remained one of his favorites, and he named it the *Rose of Poverty*.

Another breed very close to his own heart was the so-called *Mourning Violet*, a plant which would grow only when well watered with tears. Again, this oddity drew the derision of his brothers, for while these flowers did have a special beauty all their own, who had time to stand out in the garden and weep? True, the Abbot of the monastery secretly borrowed some of these seeds and planted them in a pot in his own quarters. But he could never seem to generate enough tears to get them to grow. The little window box in front of Johann's cell, on the other hand, was always brimming with violet bloom.

When next the amateur botanist produced a variety of lily-of-the-valley which flourished in barren and stony soil (where few other plants would grow), the achievement drew no attention whatsoever. And perhaps for that very reason, Johann called the plant *Meekness*.

Similarly, he received no accolades for developing a strain of wheat which produced the most wonderful-tasting bread. For the one disadvantage of this peculiar food was that, after eating it, most of the monks complained of being just as hungry as they had been before. So once again the utter impracticality of this *Wheat of Righteousness* (as Johann named it) made it the butt of many a rude joke in the monastery.

One of the monk's most intriguing experiments involved a kind of carnation, affectionately dubbed *Mercy*, whose flowers came out only in the darkest, pitch-black night. Hearing how beautiful these were, the Abbot himself was most curious to catch a glimpse of them. But after many unsuccessful attempts, he finally complained to Johann: "How can I ever see such flowers, if they only blossom at a time when it is too dark to see anything at all?"

Like his brother Gregor, Johann also did extensive work with sweet peas. Yet all that came of his years of experimenting was a strain he called *Purity*, whose only distinguishing feature was a scent so subtle that it could scarcely be detected at all. For this accomplishment, as for all his others, the humble monk was accorded nothing but criticism.

"Johann, Johann!" the Abbot chastised him. "What is the use of spending your precious days on this earth cultivating plants whose qualities can only be enjoyed by a few odd eccentrics like yourself?"

But Johann was not to be deterred. Still another of his rareties was an extremely hardy breed of grape, which he christened the *Peace Vine*. So strong and supple were the fibers of this vine that its tendrils could be braided into a superior quality of rope. The only problem was that, while tough in maturity, in its formative stages the plant was so exceedingly delicate that it required hours and hours of the most painstaking, loving care. And who but Johann Mendel had patience for such?

His sole contribution of any real practical value, as far as his fellow monks were concerned, was one which Johann himself was not much proud of. It was a type of high thornbush which, though its blossoms were sparse and scraggly, provided abundant shade, and could be grown as easily as any weed. So delighted was the Abbot with this species that he had it planted all about the monastery courtyard, so that in no time the bushes had spread throughout the grounds and were casting their cool shadows everywhere.

It was beneath a clump of these same thorns that the body of Johann Mendel found its final resting place. Although he had left behind him acres and acres of carefully groomed gardens, once he was gone these were completely neglected, for the simple reason that none of their fruits could be seen, handled, savored, or otherwise appreciated by the majority of his brothers. Only the ubiquitous thornbushes remained as the one visible, tangible product of a lifetime of toil.

After many years had gone by, however, a certain pilgrim passing through those parts was heard to make a strange observation concerning Johann's grave. Tender shoots, he claimed, of all the different varieties of plants which the younger Mendel had developed—as rare and strange and fragile as many of these were—could still be seen (by those, that is, with eyes to see) blossoming from the very earth where the body lay—even to the point of choking out the surrounding thorns!

* * *

Awake, north wind,
  and come, south wind:
Breathe over my garden,
  that its fragrance
  may spread abroad!
    Song of Songs 4:16

Stumbling Stone

AN ILLUSTRIOUS EMPEROR, troubled by the plethora of ugly idols being worshipped among the many nations in his vast domain, and wishing to further consolidate his authority, determined to establish a single state religion, unified under one supreme deity.

To this end, after consulting his wise men, he summoned together one hundred of the finest artisans from every corner of his realm: master craftsmen supremely gifted in working with jewels, precious metals, wood, cloth, or stone, and in the crafting of all manner of images. The Emperor assembled this select company one day in the Great

Hall of his palace, ostensibly for the purpose of celebrating a special festival in honor of the arts. However, having presented to each of the delegates a massive block of undressed marble, the Emperor then surprised them all by issuing a most stern decree.

Each artist was to employ his marble in the fashioning of a statue so awesome and beautiful that it would somehow express the quintessence of the Divine Nature. After one hundred days had passed, all the works were to be gathered into an exhibition and judged, and that idol which succeeded in capturing the Emperor's highest approval would then be placed amid great splendor in the sanctuary of a new imperial shrine. Henceforth, this shrine and its sacred object were to become the single focal point of all worship throughout the Empire, and every other idol would be banned. Moreover, the successful artist could look forward to being installed as the Emperor's own right-hand advisor, second in power only to himself. As for the other ninety-nine masters, both they and their works were to be summarily destroyed. The Emperor's decision would be final, and no mercy could be expected.

"Call now upon your god, every one of you!" charged the Emperor. "Let the contest begin! May each man create as though his life depended upon it—as indeed it does! And may the most powerful God of all reveal Himself, by answering one of you with His divine inspiration."

Before the initial shockwaves of this dramatic pronouncement had settled, all the artists were herded off into private "studios" in the palace Citadel (that is, they were locked away into one hundred dark dungeons), and for the next one hundred days each was left in solitary confinement, with no other company except his block of marble, a rude set of tools, and a daily ration of bread and water. Apparently, this was an Emperor who knew something of the artistic temperament: who sensed, perhaps, that the greatest products of the human spirit might emerge out of the crucible of solitude, hunger, and the imminence of death.

And so, as there was nothing else to be done, all the craftsmen set furiously to work, fashioning the grandest idols of which their hearts could conceive.

All, that is, except for one man, one artist who, unlike the others, did not set to work at all, did not so much as lift a finger. Instead, he spent all of his time simply resting on his marble block. Hour after hour, day after day, he did nothing but lie there quietly on the rock slab, his hands folded across his breast.

"Hey, have you given up the ghost already?" gibed the imperial guards as they passed his cell on their daily rounds. "What's the matter with you—can't get inspired?"

Or else they would exchange wry smiles and say to him: "So how is it going today? How is the great work progressing?"

"It is progressing," was all the man would answer.

Before long, it became a standard joke among the palace guards to observe that this man's god must be so great that the fellow could afford to wait for his stone to start carving itself.

"Say, Myron," they would kid him, "that's a pretty nice piece of work you've done. A fine job! Still, don't you think it needs a finishing touch or two?"

To which the artist would merely reply: "My work is finished."

All this while, of course, with the swiftness of a weaver's shuttle, the one hundred days were elapsing. It was almost as though Time itself were chiselling away at the lives of these one hundred artists, even as they themselves chipped at their blocks of marble.

When finally the great day arrived for the statues and their creators to be judged, all the works were brought out of the cells and set up in the Great Hall of the palace. There the Emperor, amid much pomp and ceremony, paraded from one marvelous creation to the next as each was unveiled before his eyes. Never before had such an impressive array of great masterpieces been gathered together into one place, and many were the cries of wonder and praise that arose from even the most reserved of councilors in the imperial retinue.

As for the Emperor himself, however, he remained impassive, surveying each new work with such unwavering expression that no one could have guessed his inner thoughts. Each artist stood nervously beside his own work, peering into the inscrutable jelly of the Emperor's eyes, and frantically praying that his might be the statue to capture the imperial heart.

At the same time, within every breast there burned a wild hope that this entire nightmare of a contest might somehow turn out to be ghastly ruse: that in the end all of the idols would prove acceptable, that everyone would win, and that no one would be executed. For as stern and demanding as this Emperor was known to be, could he really fail to respond with clemency to such an unparalleled display of his subjects' glorious talents? How noble was each work, and how singularly beautiful! And how perfectly obvious it was that all of them, in their own way, had been wrenched in utter integrity from the very depths of the human soul!

One artist, in fact, had been moved to give poignant expression to the common hopes and fears of the whole group, by carving his marble into the shape of a coffin, with ninety-nine doves flying out of it.

Another had made a tombstone and inscribed it with the words: "In loving memory of God."

Yet another of the sculptors had laid his block of marble on its side and fashioned a primitive but most impressive altar.

Several had carved statues of handsome youths, fully human yet godlike in every line.

Others had sculpted female figures, paragons of womanly beauty.

One artist had combined male and female into a stunning hermaphroditic form, a powerful object that was somehow both sexually and religiously alluring.

Another work depicted a pair of entwined lovers.

Still another: a newborn baby.

Some of the works were abstracts: smooth and flowing forms suggestive of breasts or eggs, clouds or flames.

Others were highly polished geometric shapes: spheres, pyramids, columns, and obelisks.

One man (rather too patronizingly, perhaps) had sculpted an image of the Emperor himself ...

And so it went, on and on, row after row of creative expressions of the quintessence of the Divine Nature.

When at length the Emperor had completed his tour of inspection, he noticed one last artist standing alone at the end of the hall, without any idol beside him. It was the man who for one hundred days had done nothing except rest on his rock.

"And where, my good fellow," inquired the Emperor, "is your contribution to this great exhibition?"

"Pardon me, Your Highness," replied this lone artist, "but I have felt my humble work to be unworthy of being shown alongside these others, and so I have left it back in my studio. Besides, if it please Your

Highness, the nature of my exhibit is such that there is really nothing to see."

"Nothing to see?" echoed the Emperor.

"That is correct, sire. My sculpture cannot be seen: It can only be experienced."

For the first time that day the Emperor's stony countenance registered a definite impression, a look not just of interest, but of positive intrigue.

"You mean to tell me," he repeated carefully, "that there is nothing about your work that can be seen with the eye?"

"There is nothing, Your Highness," replied the artist. "Even if you were to examine it closely, you would see nothing at all."

"And yet," pressed the Emperor, "you claim that this sculpture of yours can be *experienced*?"

"It can, Your Highness."

"This is very puzzling."

"Pardon my temerity, sire: But the mystery of God is great."

"Well then," responded the Emperor after some thought, "come. We must judge the work of every artist. Let us have this experience you talk about."

At that point the sculptor turned and led the Emperor, together with his entire entourage and all the other artists, out of the Great Hall and down through the long series of corridors that led to the palace Citadel, until finally they arrived before the door of the very dungeon in which the artist had been imprisoned. Here there was a suspenseful delay as the large company assembled as best they could along the narrow hall of the cellblock, cramming shoulder to shoulder amongst the torchlit shadows.

Finally the artist swung open the iron door, and paused just long enough to enable every person, by craning the neck or standing on tiptoe, to catch a glimpse inside. No one said a word.

It was the Emperor himself who was the first to break this uneasy silence.

"But there's nothing there!" he exclaimed. "The cell is empty!"

"O sire, have patience," responded the artist. "It is just as I have said: There is nothing here to be seen. Yet if it would please Your Highness to *experience* the work, I must request that you step a little closer."

The Emperor, having never once set foot inside one of his own dungeons, was hesitant.

"Have no fear, sire," said the artist. "I myself shall go ahead of you."

And so, humbly taking his Emperor by the hand, the subject stepped forward over the threshold into his cell. Just as he did so, he turned back toward the Emperor and planted a kiss upon his cheek. And at that precise moment the massive still-uncarved block of marble, which had been delicately suspended above the lintel of the doorway, came crashing down right in front of the Emperor's nose, killing the artist instantly.

Stumbling Stone

* * *

Now to you who believe, this stone is precious. But to those who do not believe ... it is 'a stone that causes men to stumble, and a rock that makes them fall.'
1 Peter 2:7-8

George and the Dragon

NOT MANY are aware of this: but after the dragon came a worm. It was the tiniest of worms, no bigger really than a hair, a downy whisker. Who would have believed that all the world's evil might hang by a mere thread?

But that's the way it was, one fine sunshiny morning, as George the dragon-slayer was taking his ease beside the castle moat. It was the day following his stunning victory over the dastardly monster that had gripped an entire village in the jaws of fear. Sir George had not yet been canonized for this celebrated coup, nor yet been named the patron saint of all England. Nevertheless, it was beginning to dawn upon him that such glorious prospects as these were not entirely outside the realm of possibility.

It had been a hard win, a grueling battle, and he deserved a rest. He deserved to revel now in luxurious exhaustion, and to savor the sweet wine of triumph. He deserved to sit for a while and enjoy a leisurely breakfast with his bare feet dangling deliciously in the cool water of the moat. And what a gorgeous morning it was for such silken repose—a morning decked out in the royal blue, the emerald green, and the shimmering gold of high summer. Indeed it was a splendid pageant of a day, almost as though the sky and the earth were vying with one another for glory on the great playing field of the world, and spangling all creation with the mystic blood of their most courteous combat.

Thus it was that Sir George, in a mood of near-perfect tranquility, reclined beside the castle moat while munching contentedly on warm muffins and scones, on fruit and jam and cider and pastries (all of which had been most daintily prepared and basketed for him by the very damsel whose life and honor he had saved on the previous day), when suddenly, just as he took his first expectant bite from a big, crisp, juicy apple, red as a heart, there in the core of it he spied ... *the worm.*

Now, this was not the first time that the would-be saint had discovered a worm in the core of an apple, and neither would it be the last. Yet the thing that was remarkable was this: that never before (at least in his recollection) had this event ever set him to such deep pondering. Who could explain the sudden power of a little molehill to assume, by overshadowing a man's entire being, the proportions of a mountain? For nestled there so cozily, and coiled like a little watch spring, this particular worm seemed somehow to have made its home not merely in the middle of a piece of fruit, but rather in the middle of halcyon summer itself, in the very heart of a day's (and dare we suggest of a damsel's?) otherwise perfect beauty, marring it.

Thus, as nearly always happens in idyllic situations, one black cloud had now intruded upon the scene. And for a single uncertain moment or two, no longer was this gallant Sir George the saint-to-be, enjoying a quiet victory breakfast beside his castle of a fine midsummer's morning. No. Instead, here was Hamlet loitering in a cold churchyard, balancing on his palm the skull of Yorick, and with it the fate and meaning of everything good in life. The simple, heroic world of romance and chivalry, in other words, had this instant been shattered by one slight hint of niggling, wiggling existentialism.

Yet just as suddenly, his sobering meditation over, the sanguine knight re-entered his own century, and blithely tossing the unfinished apple, worm and all, into the receptive waters of the moat—plunk!—he turned his attentions to a wedge of Danish pastry.

How amazed he was, therefore, to see the tiny squiggling thread of a worm come swimming back up from the bottom of the moat and begin splashing away on the surface! And not only that, but now the thing appeared to be engorging itself, as though sucking up water like a blotter, and soon was swelling with alarming rapidity to awesome proportions. In one twinkling, the slender worm had ballooned into a fat leech, and in the next, it was the size of an eel. And in no time at all there was a regular serpent thrashing around in the formerly peaceful waters of the castle moat.

By this point, of course, Sir George had leapt to his feet, rammed on his mailed boots and helmet, and girded up his sword. He was, after all, an experienced dragon-slayer by now, and he meant to dispatch this upstart handily. Curiously, as he sliced his trusty weapon threateningly through the sunlight, the glinting blade seemed more to attract this particular serpent than to repel it. Therefore, as the menacing creature glided fearlessly right up onto the stone ledge of the moat at the very feet of the adroit knight, immediately the latter brought the full weight of his boot heel crushing down upon the darting head, while at the same time dealing a single murderous blow to the middle of the slithering footless body. Which, all things considered, ought to have done the trick.

But a strange thing occurred at that juncture: For, while the death-dealing steel had certainly not missed its mark, instead of dealing death it appeared to have bounced right off the creature, almost as though this vile black body were composed not of soft flesh, but of stone. Indeed, in the very spot where the blade had struck, instantly something like a silver scale was formed. Again George struck, and again and again, sweeping his weapon back and forth in a manner that ought, by rights, to have cut his foe to ribbons. But the foe was not even scratched. On the contrary, at every blow of the sword falling amid showers of sparks like a hammer upon an anvil, a new silvery scale sprang up, until finally a shiny coat of armor plating had materialized over the entire length of the serpent's body.

Moreover, where the intrepid knight had trampled with his boot, the creature's skull, far from being unyielding, had felt so soft and malleable that it seemed to absorb the blow rather than be crushed by it, and actually to broaden out and flatten like the hood of a cobra. In fact, when once more George brought down his heel with full force, this time he saw that the strange waxlike substance of the head had retained a clear impression of his own footprint! Another stomp, and the ribbed boot sole raised a jagged mane of triangular ridges along the back of the serpent's neck. More stomps, and a wart-covered snout was formed, then a gaping maw with fangs. Thus, with each fresh impact, the malignant features grew increasingly distinct, immense, and ugly. It was almost as though the knight himself were inadvertently molding and creating this evil image, by dint of his own furious attacks upon it.

Reaching next for his lance and aiming for the tender mushroom-white underbelly, the last vulnerable spot, Sir George with one skillful thrust managed to pierce so deeply that his shining spearpoint came clear through to the other side, dripping with inky blood. Yet even then, as the knight looked on in helpless horror, he saw that the protruding ends of his shaft were puffing up like a pair of bladders, until just seconds later they virtually exploded into two gigantic, coal-black, bat-like wings, scalloped and leathery.

Panic-stricken now, George did the one thing that was left for a sensible man to do: he turned tail and fled, retreating into the castle and clanging shut the great iron door behind him. And there, quaking from head to toe in the high torchlit entrance hall, the knight leaned sweating and panting against the cold stone wall. Through a chink in the portcullis he could still see the serpent coiling and writhing out on the drawbridge, its armored body thick as a man's waist now, its head as big as that of a horse, and the wings flapping gargantuanly. Already a match in size and in fury for the dragon he had slain just the day before, this monster clearly outstripped the other in sheer magical power. What on earth was a future saint to do?

Reaching next for a crossbow, and fitting it with a long poison-tipped arrow, Sir George peered out with bated breath through his narrow portal and gingerly took aim straight into the gleaming center of the serpent's eye. Then he let fly. It was a masterful shot, but at the last moment the ghastly head veered to one side, causing the arrow to bury itself not in the eye but in the very end of the snout, where instantly it sprouted into a huge brazen horn, curved and flashing like a scimitar. And with that the enraged beast drew itself up to a towering height, lowered the enormous horn, and charged with all its might squarely against the great high door of the castle.

What happened then was something almost too horrible to be told: For far from being repelled, the hideous body somehow passed right through the sturdy door! With his own eyes, Sir George saw the heavy hulk of the monster transformed into an apparition of airy transparency, drifting like smoke through three layers of thick iron plating. Not quite invisible now, but still faintly outlined, no more was this dragon a thing of flesh and blood, but a colossal airborne phantom that seemed to fill and permeate the entire hallway. What resources had a mere man against the likes of this?

In a final desperate ploy, Sir George seized a flaming torch from a holder in the wall, and just as the ghostly monster went rushing past him like a flying mountain, he hurled the fire with all his strength deep down into the dark pit between the gaping jaws. But it was then that the most frightening transformation of all occurred: For not only did the serpent swallow the torch like a matchstick and then vomit it out in a torrent of sulfurous flames, but just as the long sinuous body came swinging round and whirling back, and just as the knight felt the first wave of its stinking heat singeing his eyebrows, precisely then the great spectral dragon, suddenly, utterly and infernally ... *vanished* into thin air! *Poof!* He was gone.

Was this cause for celebration? Was this some miraculous deliverance? Not at all. For the thing that was most dreadfully appalling about this disappearance was that in that very same moment George knew in his heart, with the kind of knowledge that is mystically branded into the soul, that the place where his enemy had disappeared to was a place not far away, but rather a place somehow even nearer than before. A place darker, deeper, and more than ever inaccessible. A place larger than any mountain, more ethereal than any flame of fire, and narrower than the edge of a sword.

So this was what that final torch, along with all of the knight's other brave and pitiful defenses, had accomplished: They had served only to purify the monster, and to put him forever beyond reach; to anneal and to cauterize him once and for all against any weapon the world could devise.

Sir George, standing all alone in the great smoky hall of his castle, sensing rather than seeing the presence of his foe, knew then without question that the thing that had begun as a tiny worm in the core of his apple was now bigger than the whole world, and completely indestructible. Moreover, the knight possessed this monstrous knowledge in his own bones, held it in his heart of hearts, felt it moving through his very veins as though his bloodstream itself were but one continuous ever-coiling serpent.

What was worse, he knew that he himself, the valiant and saintly knight, was the one responsible for this. For not only had his every stratagem produced somehow the astronomical increase of the enemy's strength, but in the heat of the battle the strength of his own arm had functioned as a kind of diabolical sculptor, creating blow-by-blow a heinous image of the very evil that, he now realized, lay within himself.

Even as he grasped this awful truth, however, and even as he felt the wickedness of the beast itself slithering around in his own innards, Sir George began to experience a mysterious transformation of his own: For staring with his mind's eye down into the depths of that secret place into which the dragon had disappeared, and feeling his whole being reel with the horror of all he saw, what else could he do then but resort to the very last weapon available to him?

What else could he do but fall upon his knees and pray?

And it was then that the knight became a saint. It was then that the Holy Spirit descended in cloven tongues of fire upon Saint George, equipping him with new and invincible weapons, endowing him with eternal power, and annealing him with holy purity in preparation for still greater battles yet to come.

For not many know this: But after the dragon came a worm. And before the saint came a sinner.

*　*　*

Put on the whole armor of God, so that you can take your stand against the devil's schemes. For our struggle is not against flesh and blood, but against the rulers, against the authorities, against the potentates of this dark world, and against the spiritual forces of evil in the heavenly realms.
Ephesians 6:11-12

Yes, Mr. Church, There Is a Jesus

IN SEPTEMBER OF 1897, a famous editorial was published in the "Question and Answer" column of *The New York Sun*. It was written by Francis Pharcellus Church, a Civil War correspondent for *The New York Times* who later joined *The Sun* as a writer specializing in "theological and controversial subjects" (which two, presumably, went hand in hand).

The question came from a little girl, Virginia O'-Hanlon, who had scrawled on a slip of pink paper the following note:

Dear Editor,
I am eight years old. Some of my friends say there is no Santa Claus. Papa says, "If you see it in *The*

Sun, it's so." Please tell me the truth: Is there a Santa Claus?

"Virginia, your little friends are wrong," came back the bold answer of Francis Pharcellus Church in the authoritative columns of *The New York Sun*. "They have been affected by the skepticism of a skeptical age. They do not believe except they see. They think that nothing can be which is not comprehensible by their little minds ..."

"*Yes, Virginia, there is a Santa Claus*," continued the legendary reply. "He exists as certainly as love and generosity and devotion exist, and you know that they abound and give to your life its highest beauty and joy. Alas! How dreary would be the world if there were no Santa Claus! It would be as dreary as if there were no Virginias ..."

So it ran, this most famous assertion of the reality of Father Christmas, and of the surpassing worth of all that he stands for. Bravo, Mr. Church! Your name has been forgotten, but your deft and eloquent handling of a controversial theological subject was destined to be immortalized in American yuletide folklore (as much as America, or yuletide, or folklore, may be said to have immortalized anything). And how many newspaper columnists may boast as much?

One can almost picture the scene, back there in old fin-de-siecle New York City, as Francis Pharcellus Church, in eye shade and arm bands, tilts back in his swivel chair with his feet cocked up on the desk, eyeing sleepily the stack of correspondence beside his old Underwood. Outside, perhaps, it's a gorgeous, sun-spangled, preposterously un-Christmassy autumn afternoon—the sort of a day when Mr. Church would much rather be stretched out on the green grass of Central Park, let's say, and soaking up some real sun, than be cooped up here in a dreary office of *The Sun* building, with the venetian blinds throwing their dusty pattern of golden bars across the faded green expanse of his desk blotter. It's the sort of a day when Santa Claus himself might have ditched his sleigh, peeled off his red suit, and headed for Coney Island.

But the world does not stop for a little sunshine. No, there are newspapers to get out, questions to be asked and answered, controversial theological subjects to be specialized in. And so, fiddling a bit with his pipe, Mr. Church sighs, pushes up his arm bands, and eventually reaches out and chooses one letter, at random, from the middle of the pile. It's a pink, squarish envelope (he's partial to missives from the fairer sex), and inside there's a single folded sheet of lined notepaper covered with the awkward, pencilled printing of a child. Even at first glance, there in the dreamy golden haze of mid-afternoon, the page seems almost to be moving, to be dancing, filled not so much with words as with tiny bony arms and legs and round, round faces in bowler hats, as though each chiseled letter were a little animated stick figure.

And that's when it happens. That's when the magic descends: the moment of inspiration, the moment that raises the hair along the back of a writer's neck ...

But wait a minute: Even granting that a certain jaded old hack may have been particularly inspired that day, his heart strangely warmed by a plea from a child—even so: Did he really have any idea of what he was about to do? Could he possibly have guessed, in his wildest dreams, that this one short article of his would somehow have the effect of distilling, for an entire culture, the fundamental significance not only of Santa Claus, but of Christmas itself? Or to go one step further: Was there the foggiest notion in the mind of this obscure journalist, that he would be the one to draft what may well be the definitive statement on the meaning of religion in contemporary Western civilization?

Or to ask a different sort of question: What if Francis Church had known that his next twenty minutes of hunting and pecking would one day be viewed by the world as vastly more important than all the rest of his life's work put together? What if he had foreseen the sort of immortality that would be his? Would the sudden, clear knowledge of such a destiny have slain him on the spot? Or might his Santa Claus, perhaps, have saved him?

But let's not get ahead of our story. Suffice it to say that Francis Pharcellus Church was not slain (at least, not that day) by a little girl's question, nor by the earnest appeal it laid upon him to tell the solemn truth. Instead, he simply snapped a clean sheet of paper into the old Underwood and rattled off his reply—*"Yes, Virginia, there is a Santa Claus"*—as the venetian blinds cast their jailbird pattern of golden stripes across his bony, gnarled fingers, and as all the elves and reindeer danced for joy. For in spite of the lure of the glorious September sunshine outside, suddenly one ragtag reporter was reminded of how much he loved sitting in this cramped office before the faded green desk blotter, and banging out answers to all of New York City's theological queries. Oh, the thrill of flattening a question mark into a period—or better still, of straightening it out into an exclamation point! And on top of that, to have one's every word backed up by such a venerable authority as *The Sun*! Yes, thought F.P.C., this was better than slogging through ditches in the Civil War ...

So much, then, for the scene in the newspaper office that historic day. But what about the other half of this quaint story? What about that other precious Rockwellian scene that would have transpired a few days earlier—the scene around the dinner table in the household of Virginia O'Hanlon and her *Sun*-worshipping Papa? As it turns out, the grown-up Virginia has herself left us an eyewitness account of it:

> "My parents did everything for me that any parents could do," she told an audience of college students some forty years later. "Quite naturally I believed in Santa Claus, for he had never disappointed me. But like you, I turned to those of my own generation, and so when less fortunate little boys and girls said there wasn't any Santa Claus, I was filled with doubts. I asked my father, and he was a little evasive on the subject.
>
> "It was a habit in our family that whenever any doubts came up as to how to pronounce a word, or some question of historical fact was in doubt, we wrote to the 'Question and Answer' column in *The New York Sun*. Father would always say, 'If you see it in *The Sun*, it's so,' and that settled the matter.
>
> " 'Well, I'm just going to write to *The Sun* and find out the real truth,' I said to father."

And that is exactly what eight-year-old Virginia O'Hanlon proceeded to do—never guessing, of course, that her innocent question was destined to make her a figure almost as famous as Santa Claus himself (or at least as famous, let's say, as Frosty the

Yes, Mr. Church, There Is a Jesus

Snowman). Neither did she suspect that henceforth her entire life was to be shadowed (or is *haunted*, perhaps, too strong a term?) by those celebrated words clacked out on the typewriter of Francis Pharcellus Church:

"Not believe in Santa Claus!" roared the great editorial. "You might as well not believe in fairies! ... No Santa Claus! Thank God, he lives, and he lives forever. A thousand years from now, Virginia, nay, ten times ten thousand years from now, he will continue to make glad the heart of childhood."

And thus it was that a chance exchange in newsprint became the stuff of immortality.

Unfortunately, in the case of poor old Mr. Church himself, it is a question of considerable theological controversy whether or not he also ended up as the stuff of immortality. For of his ultimate spiritual condition, all we can say for certain is that he died in 1906.

And Virginia O'Hanlon, who was destined to earn a Master's degree from Columbia University and a doctorate from Fordham, and to go on to a long and distinguished career as a teacher and administrator in the New York City school system, she also, lamentably, became a victim of death in 1971, at the age of 81.

As for *The New York Sun,* it died in 1950.

Death, death, death. So much of it. Alas! What would Mr. Church have to say about it, in his "Question and Answer" column, if somehow he could receive the following letter?

Dear Mr. Church:
Christmas is awfully lonely without you. But my Papa says, "Nothing's for sure except death and taxes." And he also says, "If you see something written on a gravestone, it's so." What about it, Mr. Church? Where are you now? Are you like Santa Claus, alive forever? Please tell me the truth.

Or how about dear little Virginia? Oh, to be sure, her cute Question lives on. And the famous Answer lives on, too. And love and generosity and devotion, they all, incredibly, keep on keeping on, just as Mr. Church guaranteed they would. Nevertheless, what I personally really want to know is: What about Virginia O'Hanlon *herself*, Virginia O'Hanlon the *person*? What would she have to say for herself, right now, if the grave could somehow open its dark mouth and talk? What answer would she make to the following query?

Dear Virginia:
I don't know whether this letter will ever reach you. But I need to know: If you see it in *The Sun,*

is it really so? Are you still content, in eternity, with the scintillating Answer of Francis Pharcellus Church? Are you happy up there in the North Pole, wrapped in the snowy, everlasting embrace of Santa Claus?

All this death. I can't help wondering, I suppose, what Santa himself might have to say about it all, or how he might answer this:

Dear Santa:
I'm in my 30's. Most of my big friends say there is no God, or even if there is, He's as nebulous as you are. But my minister assures me, "If you see it in the Bible, it's so." What do you think, Santa? Have you ever read the Bible? I'm writing to you because, as nebulous as you are, people seem to like you more than they do Jesus. So tell me: Is there really a God? And is He Jesus Christ? And did He rise from the dead? And is He really alive forevermore? Santa: I'm counting on you. Please tell me the truth.

* * *

If Christ has not been raised, your faith is worthless: You are still in your sins.
1 Corinthians 15:17

The Anteroom of the Royal Palace

MANY CENTURIES AGO, there lived a man who devoted his life to roaming the earth in search of all its most magnificent works of architecture. He had been to Rome, and to Athens, and to other great ancient cities, and he had gone so far (which was something unheard of in his day) as to visit the splendid temples and palaces of the Orient. Wherever there was rumored to be a grand or unusual edifice, there the traveler bent his footsteps.

Born into a family of builders, and independently wealthy, at first the man had intended to travel only for a few years, with the idea of steeping himself in the design and construction techniques of a wide variety of cultures. Yet everywhere he went, he heard stories about new wonders that lay just beyond: a fabled citadel on a mountaintop, a golden pagoda at the end of a certain road, or an entire city of green marble on the other side of a sea.

Always he found such tales irresistible, and wanderlust drew him ever onward. Like most travelers, it was not only that the new and the unknown tugged at him—it was that the old and familiar pushed him away. And disillusionment, once surrendered to, had a way of growing like cataracts over the eyes, until one day a man could wake up to find that whatever he looked at, whether new or old, was clouded over.

It was in just such a world-weary frame of mind that the traveler found himself one winter, late in life, while sojourning in a Mediterranean country. Jaded now with grand spectacles, he had come to settle in a single humble room in the one inn of a small village, where he determined to stay put for a while and try to unravel the riddle of his life. For the thought came to him hauntingly (now that his own porticoes were sagging, his own columns and foundations giving way) that man might by nature be not only a traveler, but himself a building, his every beam and stone stamped with an unquenchable yearning for permanence.

One afternoon, while sitting in the village square by the well, he chanced to fall into conversation with a peasant who was drawing water there for his sheep. As always with strangers, the traveler set

The Anteroom of the Royal Palace

about immediately to give a glowing report of his adventures, talking easily and enthusiastically about all the exotic places he had seen. (After all, if one could no longer experience real joy and wonder in life, the next best thing was to talk as though one did ...)

"Well, well," nodded the peasant, having listened attentively to the whole account. "It sounds to me as though you've seen just about everything there is to see in the whole world. And I suppose by now you've taken in our local attractions too, have you?"

"Oh yes—to be sure!" chuckled the traveler, catching the joke. "Yes, you haven't much to boast of around here, I'm afraid."

"Ah, but on the contrary," responded the peasant in apparent earnest. "Have you not seen our Royal Palace? It's right here in the village, and I can assure you there isn't anything to match it in all the world. If it's magnificence in architecture you want, then this is the thing to see."

Scratching his head, the traveler looked around at the homely little collection of plastered boxes that made up the tiny village, and at the empty rolling hills beyond. Was the old fellow daft? There was certainly no palace here. Even the largest building in sight, the inn where the traveler himself was lodging, was a mean and unimaginative structure.

Seeing his bewilderment, the peasant then beckoned with his staff and said, "Come, I'll show you. It would be a shame to have journeyed as far as you have, and to miss seeing the greatest attraction of all."

So with that, driving the sheep ahead of them, the two old men set off together through the winding laneways until they reached the very outskirts of the village. There they halted, while the guide gestured toward a little group of ramshackle outbuildings behind a row of abandoned tenements.

"There," he announced with curious finality. "There is our Royal Palace."

The traveler rubbed his eyes. Was he looking in the wrong place? But no—his new friend was pointing, unmistakably, to what appeared to be the very last and least of all the buildings in the village. Apart from a few rock doves flying in and out between cracks in the walls, the structure looked uninhabitable, unfit even for livestock. And beyond lay nothing but stubbly grainfields rising up to some desolate hills. Only the wind seemed at home here, moaning and sighing with that peculiar sound it reserved for lonely, deserted places.

The traveler, uncertain now what manner of man he might be dealing with, remarked cautiously, "It doesn't look like much from here."

"You're right," responded his guide. "From here you wouldn't know it from a hole in the ground. But what you're actually seeing is just the facade of the Royal Palace. To view the Palace itself, you have to go inside."

Accordingly, the two men went forward until they were standing right underneath the eaves of one very precarious-looking lean-to. Sunlight filtered in dusty curtains through loose boards in the roof, and the straw scattered about the bare floor was dirty and mildewed. In one gloomy back corner a door was visible, hanging half-open and askew from a single hinge. Apparently it led into an enclosed stable.

"I'll have to be about my business," advised the peasant. "But you just go on ahead and have a look around. Right through that doorway you'll find an anteroom. Wait there, and after a while you'll be attended to."

"Attended to?" inquired the traveler in surprise.

But already the old man was gathering his sheep together and herding them off along a narrow pathway that traversed the grainfields and went winding up toward the barren hills.

"I'll return for you shortly!" he called back merrily with a wave of his crook, and soon the other was left all alone with the doves, the moldy straw, the cool quiet shadows and curtains of dusty light, and the piping wind that crept ghostily through the rafters with an almost-human sound.

Well—what did he have to lose? Stepping carefully toward the back corner and swinging open the door, the visitor entered into the darker interior of what looked to be an old cowshed. Here, just a single pencil-shaft of sunlight fell through a chink in the very apex of the roof onto the earthen floor. The traveler stood very still, blinking, peering into the shadows, feeling foolish.

What in the world was he doing here? Allowing himself to be hoodwinked by an old prankster? Yet perhaps, the thought occurred to him, this might after all be a most fitting conclusion to a lifetime of futile wanderings.

As his eyes adjusted to the dim light, the first thing he noticed was an unusual knothole on the farthest wall. It was a perfectly circular mark, curiously bright, and haloed by a distinct sunburst pattern in the golden grain of the wood. Drawing closer, he began to see that the old planks held other intriguing designs too, and the longer he studied these, the more fascinating they grew. In fact, there were ferns, trees, birds, and all manner of remarkable shapes hidden amidst the swirls and ridges of the wood grain, so that all in all the effect was almost like that of a large mural. Suddenly, the odd thought crossed the observer's mind that this entire scene, taken together, gave the effect of a portrait of the original forest from which these very boards must have been cut! Not only that, but before he quite realized what was happening, the flat surface of the wall literally seemed to recede and to take on three-dimensional depth, until all at once he felt himself to be standing, incredibly, right in the middle of the green-gloom hush of a real grove of evergreens on a summer's day, with tiny songbirds threading their way through the topmost branches, and with a carpet of needles underfoot as soft and thick as the cathedralic silence all around.

Recalling with a start where he really was, the amazed visitor took a step back. But still the vision held firm, astonishingly lifelike and panoramic. Yet at the same time he found his eye wandering to a second wall, where once again the flat surface began to melt away beneath the swirling image-rich patterns of the wood grain, until now the scene that opened out to him was that of an entire mountainside drenched in the luminous gold and crimson colors of autumn, all more beautiful and vibrant than the grandest of Byzantine mosaics.

"My word!" exclaimed the traveler. "What remarkable work this is!" For already he had concluded that such glowing dioramas could not possibly be attributed to a few accidental designs in the grain of these old boards, but could only have been deliberately created by the hand of some master craftsman. What consummate workmanship was here! And all the more admirable it was for having been so cunningly concealed.

The observer was not given long to reflect on this, however, as immediately his attention was drawn to a third wall, where this time the vista unfolding before him was that of miles and miles of massive cedars, just like the great forests he had once visited in the remote regions of the north. So towering and majestic were these monoliths, they might easily have been the very columns holding up heaven itself!

But finally it was the fourth wall which turned out to contain the most wonderful tableau of all. For here, as the visitor gazed at the rude doorway through which he had first entered, in the blink of an eye he was transported bodily back to the wooded hills and valleys of his own birthplace. Once more he stood high upon a favorite lookout point, with his native city spread out below him and the sapphire ocean radiant in the distance. And again there came over him the marvelous feeling of the freshness and wonder of all the wide world, spilled out at his feet like treasure and just waiting to be explored. So full of the poignancy of nostalgia was this scene, and so charged with the shimmering magic of childhood, that it moved him to tears, and he hung his head as the memories came flooding in.

Yet even as he cast down his eyes, the very straw on which he stood was transformed in a twinkling into field upon field of ripe golden wheat, tossing in the breeze like waves and stretching to the ends of the horizon. In another direction, there appeared chains of lakes with transparent waters of turquoise and emerald, through which rainbow-colored fish glided like jeweled shadows. Elsewhere the earthen floor seemed to open wide into breathtaking canyons and gorges, studded with cataracts and clear, rushing rivers, or into flower-filled meadows or broad plains teeming with game.

As if this were not enough, when at last the traveler lifted his eyes overhead, to where the one ray of sunlight came lancing through a knothole in the very peak of the roof, here he saw that far from being a single lonely pencil-beam of light, this was none other than the sun itself, dazzling and mighty in its splendor! And here too, off among the darker slopes and rafters of the roof, shone the full moon, the planets, and all the starry host, and beyond them, unfurling out to infinity, lay the imponderable and fathomless velvet of deep space.

At this, overcome with awe, the visitor fell upon his knees and bowed his face into the musty straw. Never in all his travels had he beheld such stupendous artwork, so perfectly realistic and so full of grandeur. How was it possible?

Just at that moment, the stocky frame of his peasant friend appeared behind him, his raised shepherd's crook forming the silhouette of a question mark in the doorway. And turning toward him, the visitor implored: "Please tell me, I beg you—what place is this? And who, pray tell, is the Master Builder of this great Royal Palace?"

"Why, friend," replied the shepherd, "don't you know? You are in Bethlehem, and this is the Royal Palace of Christ the King. But listen: What you have seen so far is only the Anteroom of the Palace, and I assure you, it is nothing compared with the Throne Room! So come, won't you follow me and meet the King Himself?"

* * *

And this shall be a sign to you: You shall find the baby wrapped in swaddling clothes, and lying in a manger.
    Luke 2:12

Dreambums

THE YEAR WAS 2033, and the latest invention was a video device which recorded dreams and enabled people to play them back during waking hours.

Initially confined to the laboratory (where for some years dream research had been absorbing the energies of increasing numbers of scientists and intellectuals), dreamtech now began filtering down into popular culture.

The first public dreamhalls, plagued by radiation problems, had to be isolated in remote desert areas and were subject to heavy government regulation. Though wildly expensive, and barren of any other facilities or entertainments save the dreams themselves, nevertheless these resorts attracted hordes of wealthy patrons.

Most users agreed that sitting in a laser lightbooth, complete with panacoustic sound and a wrap-around holographic image, was a far more vivid and satisfying experience than their original dreaming had been—to say nothing of being more memorable.

With the advent of more accessible privately-owned facilities, the fad of dream-swapping arose (with all its fascinating variations), and nightmares and erotica came into great demand. The most luxurious homes, and even some private vehicles, began sporting rudimentary dream-machines—although these, in the early days, were admittedly but toys compared with the real thing.

Having long since outstripped drinking and drug-taking in popularity, dream-watching soon completely displaced sports and other mass recreations as well. In some circles, dream-interpretation and the foretelling of the future became all the rage, though for the most part audiences craved not so much to know the meaning of dreams, as simply to inhabit them.

In all the most contemporary stores, public buildings, schools, and offices, dreamscapes became an ubiquitous feature. The term *interior decoration* took on a new connotation, as experts arose with impressive skills in editing and mounting dream sequences, and in selecting appropriate material to suit mood, setting, and occasion.

A movement dubbed *Neo-Surrealism* (or more colloquially, *Avant-God*) swept the art world, as established artists began to be supplanted by a new breed comprising factory workers, young children, schizophrenics, and the like. Such obscure folk, while devoid of conventional talent, often possessed such powerful gifts for dreaming that their eerie, elegant reveries could zoom overnight to the top of the dreamcharts. Not only that, but the familiar genres of literature, music, painting, and even cinema and theatre all gradually gave way to the single spectacular artform known as Mega-Opera.

Slowly but surely, dreamtech was weaving its way into the very fabric not only of culture, but of industry, politics, economics, and practical affairs. It reached the point where dreams might almost have been described as a kind of currency, an abstract medium of exchange which not only lubricated but subtly controlled all the transactions of daily life.

If there was one development, however, which more than any other could be said to have sparked the Dream Revolution, it was the introduction of the Sleepwalker, an inexpensive portable model of dream-machine, worn over the head like a helmet. Boasting superior fidelity, this device could ensure almost total waking immersion in dreamlife.

In no time, unprecedented numbers of young and old alike were turning to an entire lifestyle of what came to be known as dreambumming. Peddling dreams for a living, and sleepwalking their way through every conceivable activity, this new species of vagabond had no other goal in life but to avoid stepping even for one second outside of the world of reverie.

Mega-operas mushroomed into unbelievably extravagant affairs, attended by millions of dream-bums and continuing for months at a time. By combining a personalized Sleepwalker with the viewing of a public show, the participant could achieve a kind of double remove from reality. All testified that the experience of marathon mega-opera was, quite simply, more real than life itself.

Of course, it had long been considered unfashionable to believe in the actual existence of anything that might legitimately be called *reality*, the *real world*, or *objective truth*. And increasingly the small minority who still clung to these antiquated terms found themselves scorned and even persecuted—especially when, in a series of famous legal precedents, the courts began shifting dramatically toward upholding the rights of dreamers.

Paradoxically, while old-fashioned notions of reality were being systematically eradicated from the mass mind, the concept of *ultra-reality* came very much into vogue, as pundits began proclaiming the veritable dawning of a new era—the so-called Age of Dreams. It was almost as though reality itself (even if it had no real existence) were on the verge of some inconceivable breakthrough into a new order.

Indeed, as if in fulfullment of this very climate of collective prophetic anticipation, it so happened that about this time the long-predicted historic event of the Second Coming occurred, and just as He had promised the Lord Jesus Christ returned to earth in a flash of lightning, splitting the sky asunder and coming on the clouds of heaven with great power and glory. However, happening as it did in the midst of so much dreaming and re-dreaming upon the earth, this cataclysmic appearing of the Son of God drew surprisingly little notice from the dream-bums.

Oh, to be sure, people paused for a moment in their helmeted Sleepwalkers, and stared up bewildered and furious at the dazzling God standing right there in front of them, just out of their reach, so near and yet so far, and all the dreamers banged their fists in a paroxysm of anguish upon the thick glass walls of their dreams. And for a while, it is true, they pulled wild and fantastic faces, literally tearing out their hair and gnashing their teeth in a futile effort to persuade the Lord of Glory to acknowledge their reality.

But as it turned out, all of these grisly antics and emotions were so similar to the prevailing ambience of the nightmares in which these multitudes had become so accustomed to living, that on the whole the transition to absolute Hell was accomplished with admirable smoothness.

* * *

Suddenly, in an instant,
  the Lord Almighty will come ...
and then it will be as it is with a dream,
  with a vision in the night—
as when a hungry man dreams that he is eating,
  but when he awakens, he is famished.
    Isaiah 29:5-8

The Last Day

WALLY WILLIS was awake before the crack of dawn. It was the first day of his retirement, the first day, indeed, of the rest of his life. This was the day he had looked forward to for over thirty years, the day he had lived for. And now he aimed to enjoy it to the hilt.

Retirement—retirement! he incanted gleefully to himself, savoring the word's magical, rejuvenescent sound. Just then, in fact, it seemed to him to be the sweetest sound in all the world, as though a mere word might possess in itself the power to make a man brand new. If Wally Willis had been a poet, he might have spontaneously composed an "Ode to Retirement." If a prophet, he might have produced ecstatic utterances.

But instead, rolling out of bed and padding downstairs for a shower, he hummed tunes from his office party of the night before: "When I'm Sixty-Four," "I've Been Working On the Railroad," "Silver Threads Among the Gold" ... Yes, he mused, ahead of him stretched his golden years. Now was the time for society to begin compensating a man for decades of faithful service on the treadmill.

With a touch of scorn, he thought of his lie-abed wife upstairs, who likely would sleep until noon. Wally had always been an early-to-bed-early-to-rise sort, and he had never understood how Molly could saw away the best part of the day, those precious morning hours. But then, he reflected, if his wife were actually in the habit of rising when he did, these hours might not be so precious anymore. Opposite sleeping patterns had probably been the great saving grace of their marriage.

Having showered and shaved, and still humming away with near-hysterical gaiety, Wally put on the coffee pot and then headed for the porch to pick up his morning newspaper. All his working life he had spent the first hour of each day poring over the paper. The leisurely ingestion of global problems was a kind of sacred ritual which somehow had the effect of cleansing and renewing him, perhaps by putting his own little troubles into perspective. And this morning, of all mornings, he decided with infinite satisfaction, these coffee and newsprint ablutions might well take two hours instead of one.

The Last Day

Yes, it was going to be a great day. Wally could feel it in his bones. What a crushing disappointment it was, therefore, when he opened the porch door only to find that for the first time since the previous year's strike, his morning paper was not in its accustomed place, draped over the clothesline.

The clothesline? Yes: Wally liked to have his paper aired out before he read it, since he found that the odor of fresh newsprint (which, as he had once learned from this very same newspaper, contained formaldehyde) always gave him a headache. How he wished he had a nickel for every time he had had to discipline a delivery boy for not hanging his paper over the line!

His first thought was that there must be a new boy. The boys were always changing, and each one had to be re-trained. Wally stepped outside and looked on the steps, the sidewalk, under the mat, all over the yard, and finally, still dressed in his bathrobe, he marched out into the street and peered up and down, searching for the boy himself. Possibly he was late.

But no—there was no sign of any boy that morning, nor any sign of a newspaper, and this turn of events hit Wally harder than any of the other items of news he might have read about that day, tragic as they would no doubt have been. For what was he to do with himself now? It was the first morning of his retirement, and he had no Plan B. For a while he simply stood on the concrete sidewalk in his bare feet, staring blankly, benumbed. It was still dark outside, and except for the eerie buzzing of a single streetlight, the entire neighborhood lay still as a cemetery.

Suddenly, coming to himself, Wally found his eyes lifting toward the hills along the horizon, attracted by some unusual activity over there. The suburb where he lived was built in a kind of bowl around the shores of a small lagoon, rising up to hills beyond. Looking now toward the eastern range, humped blackly against the pre-dawn sky like the backs of sleeping mastodons, Wally thought he could make out ... well, he knew it was preposterous ... but the more he studied these hills, the more they seemed to him to be swarming with some sort of tiny luminous creatures, like phosphorescent ants.

Heading back into the house to get his binoculars, he then went up to the third floor and slid open the patio doors onto the upper deck. From there he had an unobstructed view out over the rooftops, and as he raised the binoculars to his eyes and focussed their lenses, he spied, with startling and unmistakable clarity, something which at first glance nearly took his breath away. For yes, these hills were indeed crawling with little creatures. But the creatures were not ants. No, they were considerably larger than ants, and they looked, in fact, to be humanoid in shape. They were some sort of *men*, it appeared, and they were dressed in radiant clothing.

The Last Day

Not only that, but something like scaffolding seemed to have been erected all along the entire escarpment. Silver tubes of scaffolding in a cross-hatched pattern rose right up to the tops of the hills and beyond, while rows of the men in shining garb stood upon platforms and appeared to be doing something to the actual terrain, altering it somehow, manipulating the very rocks, the trees, the earth. Wally couldn't quite make out exactly what it was that the humanoid creatures were doing, but it was almost as though the landscape itself were some gigantic building being given a facelift.

His initial wave of surprise having passed, Wally suddenly found himself in a more objective frame of mind. What was going on here, he pondered? Was it, perhaps, an invasion? If so, it was no wonder his newspaper hadn't arrived. Returning inside, he flicked on the radio and twirled the dial. But no station would come in. Then he tried the telephone, but it too was dead. Yes, sure enough, there must be an invasion.

Strange, but this thought, once it sank in, did not cause Wally undue alarm. Naturally he was miffed about the radio, the telephone, and more than anything else, about the newspaper. But as long as these inconveniences could be attributed to an invasion, rather than to someone's incompetence, he felt he could take it all in stride. Incompetence was something he had never been able to tolerate; but this other business—well, almost anything would be an improvement over the present state of affairs.

Fixing himself a coffee, he took it out onto the deck and unfolded a lounge chair. In good weather this was his favorite morning perch. Here, high above the world, he could look out over his neighbors' rooftops to the misty black mirror of the little lagoon. The dawn air was cool and sweet, cleansed by the night, the sky darkly luminous and still spangled with stars. And like stars themselves, the distant figures in shining raiment went about their inscrutable work.

Wally sipped his coffee and studied them through the binoculars. Gradually as he did so he became more and more aware—as though swimming up by degrees out of a heavy, dream-laden sleep—that not only the hills but also the sky right above them, where the silvery dawn was just beginning to peek, was alive with whole squadrons of these same white-robed creatures. The ones higher up, moreover, appeared not to be standing upon any scaffolding at all, but rather to be hovering in mid-air, maneuvering themselves by pairs of fluttering appendages that were attached, apparently, to their backs.

Wings, muttered Wally to himself, with slow wonder. Wings. He rubbed his eyes. The figures were so far away; it was difficult to be certain. But no, unlike the creatures on the scaffolding, these ones definitely had wings, and they were flying. And now he saw that some of the wings were pure white, some

The Last Day

came in lovely pastel shades, some were shimmering gold or silver, and some iridescent. All together their fluttering made a high-pitched whirring sound like the drone of a great cloud of locusts.

Only then, in a flash, did it dawn upon Wally who these fellows really were: They were *angels*, he realized. *Angels!* Once grasped, the fact was perfectly obvious. Why then had it taken so long to sink in? But who would ever have dreamed that with his own two eyes Wally Willis would be seeing bands of angels? At the same time, it was amazing how quickly a fellow's mind could adjust to such a notion. For suddenly, it was almost as though one had been seeing angels all along, throughout one's life, and had never for an instant doubted their existence.

After that Wally began noticing long streaks of fire in the sky, like shooting stars or brightly-colored contrails, ending in bursting roostertails of sparks. And the longer he observed all these pyrotechnics through his binoculars, the more manifestly clear it became exactly what it was that these airborne crews of angels were doing: Flitting from one star to another, they were reaching out with long silver tongs and actually plucking the stars, one by one, out of the sky and then dropping them down into the middle of the little lagoon, just blocks away from Wally's home. What Wally had at first taken to be mist drifting over the water, turned out in fact to be steam, boiling up now in tremendous billows as star after star plunged sizzling into the drink. Between the loud whirring of wings, and the even louder dousing of gigantic stars, the entire atmosphere was now filled with a sound like that of armies frying bacon. And for the first time Wally caught whiffs of a peculiar odor in the air, a pungent, charred smell, as though the bacon were burning.

By this point large swatches of the eastern sky, and even a few patches directly overhead, were entirely devoid of stars. Before long fresh bands of angels appeared on the scene with swords and began cutting long incisions in the bare firmament, slashing it into neat ribbons. The strips curled up and frayed along their edges like some sort of stiff canvasy fabric, and then two angels would take hold of one end of a row and begin rolling it up, just as though packing a sleeping bag.

As long slices of dark sky were thus peeled away, Wally saw that the texture of the celestial material was not really like that of a canvas at all, but more like a kind of blubber, or the thick hide of some beast, and it even dripped with a viscid discharge resembling black blood. The angels, as if engaged in making mammoth snowmen in the sky, were accumulating huge jelly-rolls of this gory material and then trundling the bales right off the end of the horizon.

So far this amazing spectacle, while certainly most unusual, had been rather too remote and unlikely a thing to really register in Wally's mind. He had no doubt that the strange scene was, in a manner of speaking, actually and literally unfolding. But at the same time there was a kind of arm's-length quality to it, rather as though he were only reading about these events in the newspaper. All at once, however, the newly-retired man saw something which not only sank in and registered with him, but like a bolt of lighting pierced right through to the very center of his skull. For where the long strips of sky had been rolled away ... nothing remained.

Absolutely nothing.

The black, bloody substance still oozed out around the borders of the bare spaces. But the spaces themselves—they were not black, and neither were they white, nor pale, nor any color under the sun. Neither was there any sense of depth to them, nor any texture, nor anything at all. They were not even bare, exactly, not even empty. They were simply nothing.

Wally Willis had never before looked at absolutely nothing. It looked, indeed, like nothing he had ever seen in his life, and it produced a feeling in him which he had never had before, a feeling for which there was no name. It was something like dread, only slower, bigger, more ghastly and unbelievable. It was something that made not only his flesh, but his very soul within him crawl.

At this, he immediately fell on his knees and was violently sick to his stomach. Then, rising slowly and unsteadily to his feet, he groped his way back inside the house, stumbled down the darkened hallway into his wife's bedroom, and tremblingly touched her sleeping form.

"Molly? Molly?" he whispered hoarsely. "I think you ought to see this, honey ..."

But Molly was a heavy sleeper, and her only response was to grunt and roll over. Even if she were secretly awake, Wally knew, he could guess exactly what she would be thinking: Just because the old man was retired now, did that mean he was planning to make a nuisance of himself? Because if that was the case, he could just go out and find himself another job ...

Molly's cold, averted back, and the sheer hopelessness of trying to gain her interest at this ungodly hour, produced in Wally an overwhelming wave of loneliness. All the sweetness had gone out of his day. All his beloved little morning rituals lay in shambles. This day, this great day he had been awaiting for so long, this day of days had finally arrived, and now he wished that it had never come.

What was to be done? Back to the kitchen he plodded, shakily poured himself another coffee, gave it a stiff shot of brandy, and then stepped uncertainly out onto the deck again. The whole atmosphere now was indescribably eerie, hollow and bruised-looking, like something decomposed. In places overhead there were still a few bleeding shreds of sky, but they held no dawning brightness. Already it was past eight o'clock, and it was becoming painfully evident that the sun was not going to put in an appearance at all that day. With the majority of the stars now gone, and no moon in sight, the sole light came from the unearthly glow given off by the robes of the angels. Everything else was shadowy, insubstantial, as though no longer quite real.

Under such conditions, Wally was only half-surprised to notice that the hills themselves had now vanished. The angels, apparently, had completely dismantled them, until all that remained in their place was the naked scaffolding standing out starkly against the eastern horizon, like the exposed skeleton of the earth itself. It was a horrifying sight, and yet still, it was not quite as horrifying as trying to look up to where the sky had once been. The absolute nothingness there was just too much for Wally. It would have been more comforting to have the very ground ripped out from under his feet (supposing, that is, one had any choice in the matter), than to be left like this with nothing overhead.

Just at that point, however, it so happened that Wally caught sight of two of the angels right at the end of his block, just turning the corner and now striding down the center of the street toward him. These ones were of the wingless variety, yet even on foot they carried themselves with awesome majesty, as if riding upon the very clouds of heaven. They seemed to grow taller and taller with each approaching step. When finally they came to a halt, it was right in front of Wally's own house, where with a kind of ceremonial flourish they smote three times with their swords upon the immaculately-manicured lawn, causing the very ground to rumble. And then, just as their colleagues had done with the sky, these two began carving up Wally's sod and rolling it away.

"Hey!" called down the startled homeowner, surprised at his own boldness. "Hey! You guys can't do that!"

"Sorry, sir," came back the polite but official answer. "These are our orders."

As more and more of the strips of turf were sliced away, Wally saw opening up beneath them that same terrible, depthless void which already hung so inconceivably overhead. And once again just the sight of this thing, this thing that was nothing, turned his stomach upside down, and he collapsed weakly against the balcony rail.

Was there nothing he could do? At the very least, shouldn't this be reported? For some minutes, hanging over the railing, he felt paralyzed, transfixed with sickness, helplessness, incredulity. These fellows really weren't fooling, he knew. And now other angels, too, were on other lawns all over the neighborhood, and some were crawling over rooftops.

It was at this point that Wally lost his head. All his confusion, impotence, terror and rage came suddenly to a boil as he heard himself fairly shrieking, "Oh no you don't! Over my dead body! Angels or no angels, you bloody thieves aren't taking up my lawn!" And then dashing down the stairs and out into the yard, whirling his fists in a windmill of madness and whooping and shouting at the top of his lungs, just like a barrelling football player he rushed headlong at one of the men in white and hit him hard with a flying tackle to the middle. But oh! What a shock the old college linebacker got! Wally might as well have thrown himself at a block of marble or a tombstone. For like a ton of bricks he went crashing to the ground, every last atom of wind knocked out of him.

And there he lay, all morning long until noon, flat on his stomach in his bathrobe, still conscious but moving nary a muscle, while out of the corner of one mortified eye he looked on as his entire lawn, including trees, shrubs, gardens, sidewalk and fence, and the very soil beneath them, was methodically peeled off and bundled away. Eventually the angels even turned to the house itself and went to work there, using something like blackboard brushes to go over every inch of the structure and systematically rub it out, just as though it were nothing more than a child's chalk drawing. Meanwhile a third angel arrived on the scene, climbed into Wally's Oldsmobile, and drove it straight off into the Abyss.

When this third angel returned, he headed directly for the one, lone, pitifully narrow patch of sod where Wally's body still lay prone and motionless, adrift now on an ocean of nothingness.

"We'll be taking this now, sir," announced the angel, in a tone of terrifying courtesy. And lifting Wally carefully up by the hair, he flicked out this last bit of ground from beneath him, just as though kicking away a chair from under a hanged man. Next, taking hold of Wally's scalp, with one swift but surprisingly gentle motion the angel tore a strip right off him, down the middle of his face, pulling him open like a beer can. For one brief moment the victim caught sight of the appalling strip of vacuity that now divided his body cleanly in two. But then, almost immediately, following a few more deft and magisterial strokes from the angel, Wally Willis was no more ...

One moment he was, and the next moment he was not. To all appearances, he had ceased to exist ...

At least, he had ceased to exist, one might say, in quite the same manner to which he had become accustomed. For certainly it was true that he was, in a sense, *still there*. And yet in a far more overwhelmingly convincing sense, one had to admit that he was *gone*. He and everything else with him. It was all gone. There was nothing left of anything. That much was perfectly clear.

The only question was: *Where had it all gone to?*

And as for himself: *Where, what, or who was he—now that he was nowhere, nothing, and nobody?*

All he knew for certain was that his whole body still ached from his foolish flying tackle of that invincible angel. From his head to his toe he was wracked with pain. And yet, when he tried to move his head into a more comfortable position, he could not seem to find any head to move; when he wiggled his toes,

The Last Day

he discovered there were no toes to be wiggled. Even when all he wanted to do was just to moan and groan, for the life of him he could not seem to locate his tongue.

So yes, certain rather definite signs pointed to the fact that Wally Willis was, in fact, still there. He just wasn't *all* there. To his own eyes (if you could call them eyes) he appeared to be invisible. Yet at the same time he felt somehow totally exposed, naked, and very, very cold. He tried clutching his bathrobe around him, but of course, the bathrobe was gone too.

Briefly, the thought of Molly crossed his mind. Had his wife been rubbed out along with the house, he wondered? And would he ever see her again? Somehow, he knew instinctively that he would never see anything again. There was just nothing more to see. Nothing more to see *with*. No more deck to sit out on in the morning, no more leisurely cups of coffee, no more newspaper to read ...

No more news.

What, then, was left to him? In what sense, apart from this agonizing pain, could Wally Willis be said to exist at all anymore?

Well, he thought soberly, taking stock: At least I still have my *self*. They can't take that away from me ...

Yet at that point, as fate would have it, a very odd thing happened. For even though, strictly speaking, the man could not hear anything—having no ears, and there being in any case nothing to hear—nevertheless a powerful voice spoke to him out of the fathomless void, saying:

Wally Willis—you are absolutely right. No one can take away from you your self. It is the one thing you can never, ever be separated from, the one thing that is all yours, for eternity. And now, at long last, you are perfectly free to do whatever you want with that self.

* * *

All the stars of the heavens will be dissolved,
  and the sky rolled up like a scroll ...
The sword of the Lord will be bathed in blood,
  it will be covered with fat ...
For the Lord has a day of vengeance.
  Isaiah 34:4, 6, 8

Tutankhamun

WHAT IF the painstaking archaeologist Howard Carter, having dug for so many years in the Valley of the Kings, and having finally uncovered one stone step—*Eureka!*—in the barren dirt, the first of sixteen steps forming a stairway down to a sealed doorway, and from thence leading along a passageway into an antechamber filled with ancient treasures, yet also containing still another sealed doorway—

What if this Howard Carter, presuming the second door to be the entrance to the royal burial chamber, and therefore most gingerly tapping away upon it with a small hammer to make a fist-sized hole through which he might shine a light into the inner darkness, where (with any luck) no ray of light at all would have pierced for 3300 years, while hoping against hope that what he had stumbled upon would not be after all just one more empty tomb, pilfered clean centuries before by grave robbers—

What if the excited archaeologist, let's say, at this crucial point of breakthrough, instead of finding (as he certainly did) that his light illuminated a gloriously ornate wall of pure beaten gold, which turned out to be just one wall of a massive shrine nearly filling the entire inner chamber, and instead of discovering (as history undoubtedly records) yet another dazzlingly beautiful gilt shrine nestled inside the first, and within the second a third one, its golden doors embossed with a splendid relief of the winged goddess Isis, and then still a fourth shrine immaculately hidden inside the third, and all the walls of each sumptuously crafted shrine covered with elegant hieroglyphic spells promising everlasting life—

What if the triumphant Howard Carter (let's just suppose), rather than opening these final doors to unveil an immense stone sarcophagus, cool as eternity, its lid alone as impressive as the tombstone of many a famous man, and rather than lifting up this lid to discover (as countless school children now know) a breathtaking seven-foot-long coffin of delicately feathered gold foil, stunningly sculpted in the lifelike image of the boy-king Tutankhamun, with the royal crook and flail crossed upon his breast, his noble forehead crowned by the sacred cobra and vulture, his body in the shape of the god Osiris, and his wondrous face supernally serene while staring open-eyed into the ends of time—

What if the awed archaeologist, instead of later writing as he did about this hallowed moment, that "in the silence, you could almost hear the footsteps of the departing mourners"—

What if, let's say, instead of finding within this fine outer coffin a second linen-wrapped gilt coffin, one even more marvelous than the first for having been lavishly inlaid with colored glass and precious stones, and furthermore, rather than opening this second coffin to make the most amazing discovery of all—a third coffin of pure unalloyed gold weighing two hundred and twenty-two pounds, strewn with flowers still retaining their pale hues, and swathed in yards of linen embedded with gems, gold daggers, and papyrus prayers, and inside all this—like the most perfect jewel at the very center of the lotus—the celebrated, the magnificent, the incomparable solid gold mask of King Tut, surely the most wonderful ancient masterpiece that has ever come to light in the modern world, its gleaming saffron features almost more real, more beauteous, than living skin itself—

What if—just for argument's sake—what if, instead of beholding all this, and instead of then removing the priceless mask to find, smothered beneath all those layers and layers of gold, the shrivelled three-thousand-year-old mummy of the

18-year-old king himself, skinnier than a shadow now, but with his eyes still lidded as they stared out at all his lovely and comforting treasures, and with his lips still fleshed (through stretched tight in a buck-toothed simper), and with his stick arms pitifully hugging ghostly ribs as though shivering even yet with the cold of death—

What if—let's get to the point now—what if the renowned archaeologist Howard Carter, instead of discovering all these unparalleled treasures on the day when he first shone his flashlight into that fist-sized hole in the sealed door beneath the floor of the Valley of the Kings, where indeed no ray of light had pierced for over three millennia—

What if this man, this modern civilization-sanctioned grave robber, had found no gold at all in that tomb, nor anything of any worldly value whatsoever (whether materially or culturally), but instead had laid his insatiably hungry eyes upon nothing more than one single, solitary stone—and not even a semi-precious stone at that, but just the plainest, the most unpretentious, rock of granite—a big, gray boulder, noteworthy for no other reason than this:

It had been rolled away.

Rolled away from what? Ah! From the mouth of eternity!

What if, in other words, in the very place where he had fully expected to find wizened, ghastly death (along with all its golden trappings), Howard Carter had instead witnessed two men in dazzling white raiment proclaiming:

"HE IS NOT HERE—HE IS RISEN!"

Yes! What if things had turned out so?

Would such an event still have been hailed—by archaeologists, by art historians, by both the scientific and the cultural communities, by the public at large, by adventurers, by gold-lovers and by treasure-hunters the world over—as the greatest and most spectacular find in history?

* * *

Go to Pharaoh and tell him, "The Lord, the God of the Hebrews, has sent me to say to you: LET MY PEOPLE GO!"
   Exodus 7:16

Pinocchio

WHEN THE PUPPET PINOCCHIO finally made up his mind to change from being a bad, mischievous puppet into a good, obedient puppet, at that very point (so the story goes) he was transformed into a real live boy.

Now he was freed from the indignity of having his wooden nose grow embarrassingly long any time he fibbed. Instead, as a warm, flesh-and-blood person, he found that whenever he became enmeshed in the telling (or the living) of lies, a different problem beset him—and that was the constant inclination of his living humanity to revert, little by little, to its original state as a block of wood.

At first it was only in the most trivial ways that this tendency announced itself. A bright boy full of energy, Pinocchio sailed through high school and university. Not until the day he marched up on stage to receive his Bachelor's diploma did he become aware of a certain leprous, parchment-like substance that was spreading like papery fur over his fingernails. Soon after that, the nails stopped growing altogether, thickened, and lignified. Though initially all this meant to the youth was that he was relieved of having to cut them anymore, their unsightliness made him increasingly self-conscious, to the point where he took to wearing gloves whenever he went out.

An even more bothersome disorder, however, arose during his first year of post-graduate studies, when he began having trouble with moss growing between his toes. He now found that if he stood for too long in one place, it could be difficult to get his feet unstuck.

The next area to be affected was Pinocchio's forehead, which gradually assumed a furrowed, barky appearance, and in time went hard as a stump. Not only that, but the young man felt his powers of concentration waning until eventually, having lost all capacity for studying, he made the decision to quit school and enter the business world.

Here he made speedy progress, advancing soon into a suite of oak-panelled offices where he spent his days sitting around the board table and shuffling stacks of paper. Unfortunately, so surrounded was he now by forest products that before long the skin all over his body began to take on a calloused, grainy texture, almost as if woodenness were a quality which could seep into the pores by osmosis.

Furthermore, like most of his colleagues, at this stage in life Pinocchio felt little attraction anymore toward his wife, who did not understand him at all. One day, while ogling another woman in the office, the young executive heard an odd clicking noise in his eyelids, and within a week he found to his wide-eyed astonishment that his eyeballs had frozen solid in their sockets! No longer was he able to blink, and whenever he wanted to look at a woman now he had to turn his entire head. While this did nothing to curb his lust, it did extract some of the dignity from it.

Accordingly, in hopes of somehow loosening up, Pinocchio began to throw himself into worthwhile community activities. He joined a local fraternal order, volunteered his fund-raising skills to various benevolent causes, and frequented a posh country club where he could take some exercise with likeminded humanitarian gentlemen. To his distress, however, he found that on the links his legs and arms tended to stiffen right up like the shafts of his clubs, so that at the end of eighteen holes, it would be all he could do to unlock his knees and bend his elbow for the nineteenth. Moreover, his handling of charitable funds, strange to say, seemed only to exacerbate a nasty arthritic condition in his hands, which in time rendered them gnarled and woody as tree roots. As for the fraternal order he joined, who would have guessed that a fellow could go on functioning in a more or less normal fashion (let alone stay alive at all) after his very heart had petrified into a cold, hard little billiard ball?

By this point Pinocchio's bizarre condition was causing him not only physical discomfort and inconvenience, but a good deal of internal anguish as well. Unwilling to seek help, however, the more he bottled (or boxed) things up inside, the more wooden he became, and the less capable of expressing or even identifying his pain. It was as though suppressed feelings were a kind of cold, sap-like blood which ran more and more slowly and sluggishly, until finally it clotted to a standstill.

Gepetto, Pinocchio's creator, watching this grim process at work in his beloved puppet, became increasingly troubled. How well the old craftsman remembered the day when his little mannequin had sprung to life, becoming a real-live child before his eyes! For was it not in that same glorious moment that he himself had become a true father, with a longed-for son to call his own? But now, as time wore on and Pinocchio's visits home grew fewer and farther between, the forlorn Geppetto was again left feeling that he was no real father at all, but only an aging and deluded toymaker, the mere constructor of a heartless puppet.

Meanwhile, in a desperate bid to try and make something of himself, Pinocchio determined to toss his hat into the political ring and run for mayor of his city. After all, he was a well-respected man, with a high public profile, and who but Geppetto knew how close he was to being a total blockhead?

No sooner was the campaign underway, however, than Pinocchio's condition took an alarming turn for the worse. He noticed it first in his neck, which one morning he was unable to turn either to the right or to the left (even to leer at a pretty girl). Then his bulbous nose stiffened up into a shiny button, his jowled cheeks became like burls, and his two little ears went hard as pine knots. Naturally, none of this prevented the dapper Pinocchio from winning his election handily. But by the time it was all over, he found that his face was no longer capable of forming any expression whatsoever, save the one pasteboard smile that had been plastered all over town on his campaign posters. The only place he retained any movement at all now was in his mouth, which he could still wag crudely up and down with a square, hinged, nutcracker-like motion.

After three terms in office, despite undimmed popularity Pinocchio was forced into early retirement by his crippling affliction. At this stage he was so far gone that there was little else for old Geppetto to do but to set the poor fellow back on his shelf in the workshop, and try to keep him comfortable. There for several more years the celebrated politician and financier sat prattling away about all his exploits, milking whatever meager enjoyment he could from his last ounce of animate human flesh, his tongue. Often this idle chatter caused his maker to wonder whether any true spark of genuine humanity could possibly be left inside him. Day after day the creator remonstrated with his creature, pleading with him to at least clean up his language and refrain from telling so many bald-faced lies. For once again the wooden nose had begun to grow—so long now, in fact, that it was bending and coiling around the room like a snake.

"My dear Pinocchio!" admonished the wise old man one day, after the nose had tied itself into an excruciating knot. "Lying has become your native language! It's all you know how to do! But if only you could speak one solid word of truth, even now there might yet be hope for you!"

"What is truth?" replied the puppet in a voice like sawdust, as his nose lurched forward. And that very moment, while the horrified Geppetto looked on, the nutcracker jaw closed for the final time, sliding shut like a coffin lid over the empty black hole of the square little mouth.

And Pinocchio, whether as puppet or as man, was never heard from again.

* * *

Idols have mouths, but cannot speak,
eyes, but they cannot see;
ears have they but they cannot hear,
hands, but they cannot feel ...
All those who trust in them will become like them.
Psalm 115:5-8

And His Train Filled the Temple

A CELEBRATED POPULAR THEOLOGIAN had three desks in his study.

At one desk he worked from Monday to Wednesday writing the concise, lucid Bible commentaries for which he had become so well known. This desk was the largest of the three, a massive old thing of oak situated in a bay window with a lovely view of the English countryside. It was a most fitting place for reflecting upon eternal truths, and for putting those truths into a plain man's language.

But the writer had a second passion besides theology, and that was trains. One entire wall of his study was covered with photographs of famous locomotives, and against this wall was positioned his second desk, where every Thursday and Friday the theologian donned an engineer's cap (literally) and sat down to write books about trains. He had produced a scholarly account of English railroading, a history of the caboose, an encyclopedia of train lore, and several other volumes, all of which he published under a pseudonym.

It was the third desk in this author's study, however, which was in some ways the most curious one, for it was a wooden school desk, small and homely, of the old sort with a hole for an ink bottle in one corner and the surfaces deeply engraved with generations of graffiti. Here every Saturday the theologian lowered his ample frame carefully into the tiny wooden chair and, with his knees bunched up against the bottom of the desk, wrote children's stories. The cramped position helped him, he always said, to think like a child—something admittedly not always easy for a celebrated theologian.

With his three desks, then, and his three passionate interests, and his three distinct reputations, the theologian might easily have been three different people rolled into one—a kind of mirror of the great Trinitarian mystery he so loved to write about. There were many readers, in fact, who knew the author only by his train books, and had no idea that he also wrote theology. Many more were familiar with his theology but had never read his children's stories. And so on.

For the writer himself, however, the boundaries between these three identities and areas of work were not always so clear-cut. The commentaries, for example, were filled with illustrations and stories so simple that a child could understand them. And when mulling over a problem in theology, it was not unusual for the writer to step outside and take a stroll down to the railroad tracks, about a mile from his home. Sometimes while he was there a train would go rushing by, and then he would stand as close to it as he possibly could—just like any daredevil young lad—letting the noise and the wind and the rumble of it course through his body from head to toe. For often enough, in the strange and sudden vacuum of stillness that always hung like a struck gong in the wake of the caboose, the theologian would hear answers to deep questions.

By the same token, the very act of creating a children's story might have the effect of raising these same questions all over again, yet this time in such a way that the questions themselves would seem answer enough.

So the boundaries of the writer's work tended to get blurred—just as standing with one's nose in the wind of a speeding train could have the effect of blending ninety-nine multi-colored boxcars into a single entity—and that was why he found it helpful to use three separate desks for keeping track of his various projects. After three days of expository theology, he was quite happy to get back to his trains. And after two days of trains, a Saturday of stories, and a sabbath of rest, by Monday morning he was ready once again to tackle his Bible commentaries.

Each desk was piled high with the accumulated manuscript pages of its own work-in-progress. And each was equipped with its peculiar set of tools: for the children's books, a pencil and scribbler; for the trains, an old black Underwood; and for the more rarefied work of theologizing, a personal computer with the latest word-processing and biblical-reference software.

Thus the week would go by—sentence by sentence, desk by desk, book by book. It was a well-ordered, literary sort of life.

Late in his career, however, one Saturday in spring, an unusual occurrence befell the theologian—something which at first appeared to throw his carefully-disciplined existence into total chaos. Seated at his little school desk that morning, knees bunched, trying to think like a child but finding himself preoccupied instead with a problem in theology, he found himself at the same time perking up his ears to listen nostalgically to his favorite sound in the world: the distant, mournfully-ecstatic wail of a train whistle. It was a balmy, daydreamy sort of day and the casement windows of the study were thrown wide open so that the beautiful, wild sound came drifting into the room and tugged at something inexpressibly deep in the theologian's soul. What was it about this sound? Somehow it seemed to sum up all questions, all answers, all the earth's yearning and heaven's reply. It was as though the archangel Michael were a black jazz musician playing, not a trumpet, but a saxophone! The single sustained note came rhapsodically out of the far distance, and disappeared into the distance again. Heard for a few passionate moments, then gone.

And now, just at that mystical point when the sound itself was all but lost (so that one could not say with certainty whether it still could be heard, or whether what was heard was but the memory of it, or perhaps only the sound of the distance itself), just then, out of nowhere, a wind blew up. First a few fingers of breeze poked into the study and rustled about, like an unseen hand ruffling a child's hair. Then came an abrupt gust that picked up a sheaf of computer paper from the big oak desk and sent its fanfolded streamers flapping all about the room like a startled flock of papery-winged pigeons.

Reluctantly, the theologian got up to close the big front windows and to set about sorting the scattered sheets. But immediately there came another gust through a side window, this time a stronger one that swept across the train desk, lifting an entire book manuscript up into the air and blowing it around like a cloud of dead leaves. And all at once there was a regular gale in progress, right there in the study, so that it was all the elderly writer could do to lean against the force of this great unearthly wind and to struggle to get his windows closed on all three walls.

Yet even when he accomplished this, somehow the violent wind kept blowing, eerily and unabated, just as though it were trapped now within the house. Outside all seemed calm, but inside raged a howling storm of paper, white and blinding as a blizzard. Books were dumped from their shelves and pages torn loose, the precious pictures of locomotives came rattling off the far wall, and even the three filing cabinets toppled over and spilled their entire contents into the whirlwind. All the owner's frantic efforts to restore order were in vain, and in utter helplessness he looked on as train stories, children's writing, and theology all got jumbled together and strewn every which way. Finally there was nothing he could do but to lie down flat on the floor with his hands over his head, to protect himself from being sliced to ribbons by his own knife-edged creations.

It was then, out of the corner of his eye, that he saw the strangest sight of all: for not only his papers were being blown around, but the writing itself, the very print upon the pages! Individual letters were being detached from their moorings and, still intact, were bouncing all over the room like black hailstones! At that tumultuous point the writer lost consciousness, sinking away into a dream-filled sleep in which he saw himself wandering knee-deep through an endless slough of alphabet soup, a pepper-and-salt wilderness of uninterpretable, glossolalic print ...

When he awoke, it was Sunday morning and the room was calm once more. Not only that, but all of the chaos of the day before had been miraculously swept away, whisked clean, and now bright sunlight streamed in through the tall windows upon a perfectly tranquil and well-ordered scene. True, the familiar books and papers and pictures and furniture, including the three beloved desks, were now gone, vanished into thin air. All that was left in their place was a single plain table in the middle of the room, like a simple altar. And upon this altar, bathed richly in the sunlight, lay a large and beautiful book.

At first sight, the theologian assumed this book to be a Bible, as it was a most impressive volume, sumptuously bound in gold. Yet as he got to his feet and drew nearer to investigate, he was surprised to see his own name embossed on the jewel-studded cover. Nothing else: only his name. Strangely, this detail reminded him of the four Gospels: Matthew, Mark, Luke, John. And the great prophets: Isaiah, Jeremiah, Ezekiel.

What better title for a book, whispered a voice inside him, *than simply the name of its author?* Indeed, as he opened the golden tome and began to leaf through it, he saw with astonishment that it did contain all his very own writing! Everywhere he turned familiar thoughts and phrases leaped out at him—though how exactly he managed to recognize it all he could not say for sure, as everything seemed slightly askew, altered somehow, transformed. Sentences and whole paragraphs of theology, for example, had been lifted out and inserted into other works; obscure information on railroading had somehow found its way into the children's stories; and passages from the latter had been interfiled with the Bible commentaries. Nevertheless, it was all there—all the scriptural expositions and the stories and the train lore, every last word he had ever written. And while none of it was in quite the same order as his original, the author was dumbfounded to discover that far from appearing a hopeless jumble, this new revised version seemed to express things exactly as he had always longed to express them. It was just what he had wanted to say all along!

With tears of joy the truth came home to him: that his entire life's work had been edited, polished, transfigured, and seamlessly amalgamated into a single magnificent magnum opus. And so, falling on his knees in wonder, he turned back to page one and commenced to read more carefully, cherishing each and every word of the glorious new style:

"*Once upon an eternity*," read the opening sentence, "*I saw the Lord, and His train filled the temple ...*"

* ✲ *

*As you do not know the path of the wind,
or how the body is formed in a mother's womb,
so you cannot understand the work of God,
the Author of all things.*
　　Ecclesiastes 11:5

The Time Machine

I

THE TIME MACHINE—sleek, gangly, tubular, garish, gleaming—sat in Herbert George's garage. It looked like some sort of computerized still, a cross between the latest technology and something as old as the hills.

Herbert George had poured a lifetime into perfecting it. The early stages of the project had been particularly taxing and difficult, since for many years the inventor had been unable to escape the narrow boundaries of the day at hand. At one o'clock in the afternoon, for example, he would set out for the Renaissance, only to have the machine take a nose dive and dump him back at eight o'clock that same morning. It just wasn't very exciting being given a chance to eat his breakfast again and to tighten the same set of bolts twice in one day.

On top of that, there was the perennial problem of trying to spring himself back into the present. Many a time Herbert had lost his way completely, and had ended up *hiccoughing* (as he called it) back and forth between morning and evening, or even bouncing around from one minute to another. The plain fact was, that ever since those earliest experiments the time traveler had never been quite certain as to whether or not he had actually found his way precisely back into the present moment. Once you started fiddling with the mechanism of time, the whole works got slippery as a greased pig. Hiccoughing became a way of life.

The inventor's years of frustration had finally paid off, however. For one day when he had set the controls and floored the decelerator, in the blink of an eye he found himself transported back to an English concert hall in the eighteenth century, where a performance of Handel's *Messiah* was in progress. Herbert adored Handel, and the *Messiah* especially sent him into raptures. So when the King himself rose to his feet for the *Hallelujah Chorus*, and the entire audience with him, Herbert too stood at attention beside his machine and shivered with ecstasy. It was almost like dying and going to heaven.

Consequently, when he woke up the following morning on the floor of his own dingy garage (having somehow groped his way back there), all Herbert could think about was setting off on another voyage. Indeed, the time-travel bug had bitten him more deeply than ever now, and even as he strolled down to the café for breakfast that morning, the bright sunshine of this brand new day appeared to his eyes dull, already faded, and pitifully unglamorous.

Today, today, he lamented: It was *always* today. How confining it was! But now at long last Herbert George felt his hand upon the very trigger of time, and he saw the whole of history stretched out beneath his feet like a magic carpet.

Because of his love for the arts, he began by visiting celebrated cultural events. He watched Michelangelo at work on the Sistine Ceiling. He attended Tutankhamun's funeral, and looked in on the Athenian Temple of Venus in its heyday. He was present when Socrates drank the cup of hemlock, and he sat with Monet during his painting of the Cathedral of Rouens in all its changing lights. He also witnessed the death of Tolstoy in the little train station at Astapovo, and, while in the vicinity of that decade, just for fun he dropped in to see the riot at the first performance of Stravinsky's *Rite of Spring*.

This latter experience whetted his appetite for crowd scenes, and in turn for revolutions, assassinations, and the like. And from there he progressed to great battles and atrocities. There was something fascinating about bloodbaths, about watching human beings behave like animals. Herbert developed a special interest in attending the Roman Colosseum, where it seemed to him that the conflict in the arena somehow caught the very spirit of the soul of history. Having done his Ph.D. in the field of art history, he had always believed that the arts were the decisive influence upon the course of civilization. But now he began leaning toward the theory that the central and more basic catalyst was violence.

It was in this way that the cultured time traveler gradually found himself exploring hungers and curiosities which, frankly, went somewhat beyond the bounds of purely cultural or historical interest. How many sweet hours, for example, did he while away spying upon the likes of Cleopatra and Helen of Troy in their boudoirs? Not that such women were really very beautiful. No, it was another quality altogether which they possessed, something more riveting, and somehow more decadent, than mere sex appeal. Perhaps, reflected the traveler, in the long run it was not even art or violence, but *decadence* that turned the wheel of time and was the true lifeblood of history.

For Herbert George himself, the splendid panorama of the past had begun to function almost as a kind of drug, a goblet brimming with ambrosial liquor. He would actually awaken from his journeys with a pounding headache, and with fur lining his mouth, just as though he had spent the night carousing. And since much of his time at home now was taken up with sleeping off these wretched hangovers, he came to view the present more than ever as something disagreeable, as an illness to be avoided like the plague: just one long, miserable bout with jet lag.

Another problem with the time machine was that none of the famous figures of history ever seemed to take the slightest interest in the inventor or his device, let alone to enter into conversation with him. Inexplicably, Herbert found himself strictly confined to being a mere onlooker, an ethereal observer rather than a full-blooded participant in the past. This meant that being physically present at the great moments of history was, after all, not very much different from viewing a motion picture.

Of course, this drawback also had its advantages. It wouldn't have done to have had his machine literally stampeded by Hannibal's elephants! Nevertheless, this enforced detachment from all the events he witnessed gave Herbert a rather eerie, ghostlike feeling, and over time left a gathering sediment of ennui. Things might have been different had he felt at home in the present, or had he at least had *some* place (or rather, some *time*) where he could go and let down his hair, and simply be himself. But gradually he began to wonder whether he might have abrogated his right to be a real citizen of any era at all, becoming instead a mere spectral wanderer down the corridors of the eons. Just because all doors were open to him, there was a sense in which all were now closed, and there came a point at which living in two dimensions of time seemed almost more confining than living in just one. This was a wrinkle which the resourceful inventor would have to work out.

Increasingly, therefore, Herbert George came to pin his hopes upon breaking the barrier into the third dimension of time, the future. For although he had tried every angle on it, this was the one door which still remained locked to him. He had even conceived the plan of going right back to the beginning of the universe, theorizing that this might prove paradoxically to be the secret passageway into the future. But this was an enormously ambitious undertaking, and who could say whether a man might ever return at all from such a journey?

Meanwhile, Herbert had begun to be plagued by yet another, entirely new problem, and this was the nagging suspicion that perhaps the real barrier to be broken might not be time at all, but *reality*.

II

One day, on a fairly routine jaunt, the traveler packed a lunch and set off to see Jesus of Nazareth. It was one of those trips he had been planning for some while but had just never gotten around to. Somehow it seemed too obvious a thing, too touristy, like going to Disneyland. Besides, Herbert wasn't quite sure exactly what event he wanted to witness in this controversial man's career. There would be no sense in listening to the Sermon on the Mount, for instance, as he wouldn't understand a word of it. And what attraction would the Crucifixion hold for someone who could have a ringside seat at the Colosseum any time he wished? As for the Resurrection, Herbert doubted whether there would really be anything to *see*. Even the Roman guards at the tomb, after all, who were the sole eyewitnesses, had apparently not believed in it.

"Still," mused the traveler one day, "it would be hard to beat a good raising from the dead." And so, more or less by a process of elimination, he decided to content himself with the scene of Lazarus emerging from the tomb. Would the fellow really be wrapped up tight in linens, he wondered, and come out like a walking mummy? Not that Herbert expected, with his scientific turn of mind, to be convinced of anything. But it would be an experience all the same. It would be something just to see the famous Wonderworker in action.

Thus it happened that one quiet Sunday morning the intrepid pilot sat his controls, pressed the decelerator, and sat back to watch the usual tunnel-like blur of the centuries flying past his window. In moments he found himself translated back into a land which, though he had never set foot there before, bore a striking sense of déjà-vu about it. How to explain this, precisely, Herbert couldn't say. But the stony hillocks, the dusty tufts of grass, the few scrubby-looking trees, the very color of the soil itself, faded and crumbly: all this had the look of some old, lost childhood book, the pages of which had been turned, smeared, frayed, and all but obliterated with familiarity.

At the same time, the traveler could not help but be aware of a somewhat alien quality to the place, a certain strange tint in the atmosphere. Even the gentle breeze upon his cheek had an odd, papery feel, a raspy touch that he had never quite experienced anywhere else. Not that this was the first time he had encountered such phenomena on his trips: Indeed, it seemed that every age had a slightly different aura about it, a climate and a texture all its own. This was something that went much deeper than mere changes in geography or human culture, and that defied analysis. It was almost as if the very sun, in different centuries, were a different sun, another star altogether, or as if the earth itself might ebb and flow like the tides. One would have thought that such things as the wind and the rain would remain constant. But no, even nature seemed subject to subtle alterations, as though she herself were growing old, or else being continually renewed.

The time machine had come to rest at the bottom of a broad, shallow, quarry-like depression. All around were walls and shelves of pinkish, powdery rock, just low enough for the observer to be able to see over the lip to a few barren hilltops and sparse clumps of trees in the distance. It was a hot bright day, approaching noon, and not a soul was in sight. Initially Herbert was puzzled, since by now he had learned to land his machine with extreme precision, and he had expected to see Jesus. But then it dawned on him: This would be the local cemetery, the place of tombs. Looking about he could see where roundish boulders had been rolled against the mouths of small caves hollowed out in the cliffs. A few of the caves, apparently empty, were as yet unsealed, and their openings yawned darkly, blue-shadowed against the pink.

Herbert George stood very still beside his vehicle, his thoughts vague, dislocated. He knew he must be in Judea in the first century. And yet the desertedness of the place, the godforsaken desolation, the concentrated heat, the tombs, all this made for a sense of timelessness, an eerie feeling of centuries slipping away beneath the feet like broken shale. The visitor might literally have been standing at the end of the world, peering over the crumbling edge. All that seemed certain here, it occurred to him, was the presence of death itself, a presence somehow both final and unsettled.

Having waited and watched for some time like this in the unnerving, straight-jawed, mideastern sun, on a sudden impulse Herbert made up his mind to leave, to abandon this particular project, perhaps to return another day. In fact, he had even gone so far as to swing back into the saddle and to have his hands on the controls of the machine, when all at once he caught sight of a group of figures in the distance. They appeared briefly over the brow of a little hill, sank out of view, then reappeared abruptly at the very edge of the escarpment, their forms darkly opaque against the brilliant sky. They were a fairly large group, and more and more figures kept arriving on the scene and fanning out around the lip of the quarry. It seemed a great many people for so lonely a spot.

As always in such situations, the traveler's immediate impression was one of unreality, of something so preposterous as to be fraudulent, as if this were no more than a crowd of Sunday school children garbed in terrycloth bath towels, or a bunch of Hollywood actors gathering for a scene. It was the old curse of celluloid vacuity which haunted, increasingly, all of Herbert's trips. And now his mind, with typical twentieth-century skittishness, began to hop back and forth between an entirely inappropriate mood of zany vaudevillian comedy, and a due sense of the most somber gravity of what he knew was about to take place.

Having climbed out of the machine by now, he scanned the distant faces looped in their stripey hoods, trying to pick out the One he had come to see. *Yes—there He was!* That surely was He, head bowed, in conversation with the two women. Herbert's heart quickened. This was a smaller man than one would have expected. He did not stand out. There was no radiance about Him. What was it, then, that was so unmistakably recognizable, and so compelling? For all at once the time traveler, this veteran of the spectacular, felt himself filling up with such an unaccustomed rush of feeling that he wanted to shrug it off somehow, to laugh it off, to turn to a friend and make some frivolous, sarcastic comment. He steadied himself against the frame of the machine. The Christ was speaking, nodding His head. He was nearly, yet not quite, within earshot.

Just then the traveler distinctly saw one of the women at Jesus' side extend an arm and actually point in Herbert's direction. And the very next moment he saw the face of the Christ suddenly contort, and break into sobs—horrible, wrenching sobs so violent that the man's whole body shook, and the sound of His weeping carried throughout the quarry and echoed against the stone walls, almost as if the rocks themselves were crying. At that, Herbert George recalled the one single Bible verse which, for some reason, he had ever known: *"Jesus wept."*

Indeed, if he hadn't known better, the traveler might have assumed that the woman at Jesus' side had been pointing directly at himself and at his strange device—as though *he* were the one somehow responsible for the Christ's tears. By now, however, he was well accustomed to the fact that in the eyes of the past both he and his machine were entirely invisible. There had even been occasions when the personages of history had actually walked right through him, showing not the slightest awareness of his presence—an event which always left Herbert feeling somewhat queasy, and pondering: Which one of them was the ghost?

Even so, as the weeping man detached himself now from the crowd and began to pick His way along the steep winding path that led down to the tombs, right down to where Herbert was, the latter had to do a double-take. He had to remind himself vigorously that, even to the eyes of Jesus Christ, he was indeed invisible, shielded by a barrier of twenty centuries. For the fact of the matter was, never before had the traveler received such an uncanny impression of an actor, as it were, stepping right out of the screen of history, and becoming living flesh before his eyes. The man was simply riveting, and on impulse Herbert held up his own hand in front of his face, as if to check that he himself was still there. For somehow the sense of his own reality seemed to flicker and pale before the coming of this man Jesus. *Which one of them was the ghost?*

The Christ had now reached the floor of the quarry, and was walking directly toward him. He would be heading, Herbert tried to remind himself, for the tomb of Lazarus, and cautiously he glanced over his shoulder to see if he could spot which tomb this might be. The pink cliffs blazed behind him, as though on fire. And Jesus kept coming. He looked three-, four-, no, *seven*-dimensional.

It was high noon, yet all at once Herbert felt cold and shivery, as clammy as clay. Then his mind did another of its bizarre flip-flops, as for one instant he pictured Jesus and himself as two rivals locked in a kind of extraterrestrial duel, combatants facing each other now in a showdown on the stony flats of an alien solar system.

Jesus kept coming. A cosmic jouster, an intergalactic gunslinger, yet with eyes maddeningly human, eyes still wet with tears. Eyes that probed deep and meltingly into the very heart of Herbert George. Almost right on top of him now. Would He walk straight through him?

But no: the unthinkable was happening.

Their eyes were meeting ... locking.

Jesus—there was no shadow of doubt about it now—Jesus *saw* him!

Herbert George winced, cringed, shrank under the shock of this unprecedented exposure.

And now the Christ was opening His mouth and was speaking to him, in words that were like the erupting of a volcano inside him: *Herbert George, do you love Me? Will you leave your machine, and come with Me ... ?*

Herbert writhed, looked away. He wanted to crawl into a hole. Had the words, perhaps, been addressed to someone else? But no, there was no one else. Jesus Christ had called him by name.

He wanted to blurt out—"Hey! You can't do that! You can't talk to me like that! Don't you know there's two thousand years between us?"

But he couldn't find his tongue. He could no more speak, it seemed, than fly. Then all at once he remembered his machine: Even now his trembling hands were gripping the tubular chassis, making the whole frame shake and rattle like a heap of metal bones. And suddenly, nearly jumping out of his skin with panic, Herbert yanked himself up into the saddle, hit the controls, and rammed his foot to the floor. With a violent quake the time machine went lurching away from the earth, as for one final, tremulous instant the frightened pilot saw the face of Jesus framed against the pinkish rock, streaming tears. Then above the blast of the engines he clearly heard the roar of the Lord's voice, a resounding boom that echoed all around as though ricocheting from one end of the universe to the other—

"LAZARUS, COME OUT!"

III

Too shaken to know what he was doing or where he was going, Herbert sat stupefied as centuries of stars and eons of deep empty space flew past his port window. The cabin pitched and yawed alarmingly, charging forward more like a runaway horse than a mechanical thing, as though possessed of a will of its own. No more could the inventor control his invention now than he could control his own wild emotions.

"You've got to get hold of yourself!" he stammered, but he couldn't get hold of anything. He thought he had had bad trips before—times when, utterly disoriented, he hadn't had a clue how to find his way home again. But this was something else. Now time itself seemed to have him by the scruff of the neck and to be shaking the living daylights out of him. Stars filled his eyes, detonating like flaming arrows against the windshield, and then he began seeing sunrises—not rosy and beautiful ones, but red and enormous and angry, like open wounds in heaven itself—as over and over again the sun rose, and faster and faster, until finally there was nothing at all but sunrise, nothing but a gigantic orb of eternally erupting fire right in front of the terrified pilot's eyes.

It was, therefore, with profound surprise and relief that just moments later Herbert George found himself at home once again, in his own ordinary little garage, lying flat on his back on the cool concrete floor as though stretched out on a slab. And there right beside him was his precious machine, sleek and intact, with not a scratch on her gleaming metallic hide.

Thanking his lucky stars for this safe landing, the traveler rose carefully to his feet and dusted himself off. He was a little stiff, yet still in one piece. Of course, he had his usual hangover headache, together with a thirst so parching that his throat felt like an hourglass with all the sand of the Sahara Desert running through it. How hot and dusty it had been in that wretched Holy Land! Entering the house, he pointed himself straight toward the kitchen, where the stainless steel faucets smiled at him a toothy, twentieth-century welcome.

However, when he tried turning the water on, nothing came out. Not even one little drop. The shiny wink of chrome might as well have been a mirage on the burning sand. What a time for the water to be off! Yet more serious than that, when he turned to his refrigerator and swung open the great white door, there was nothing in there either. Not so much as a can of frozen juice. Nothing at all. Nothing but the cool, quiet, electric brightness of the blank interior.

Herbert stared, open-mouthed, almost as if he were watching something unbelievable on television. And then in a flash of absurdity, his mind formed one of its bizarre and disconnected images: He saw a team of pallbearers on skates, dressed in white tuxedos, carrying his refrigerator in graceful, gliding procession across the endless glassy ice of the moon.

After that, things got progressively zany. For glancing out the kitchen window, Herbert noticed that the sky was red, and then, peering more closely, he saw that not only was it red—it was bloody. The entire sky was awash and running with blood, just as though some monstrous wild animal had raked its claws repeatedly over a soft flank of warm flesh. It was broad daylight, and yet the light was somehow not that of day at all, but of night—lurid and appalling, with everything stained and distorted by the dark luminosity of blood.

Trembling violently, Herbert began running throughout the house, frantically checking every faucet, paranoidally eyeing all the windows. And as he ran the house itself vibrated, shuddering ominously under every footfall. At wits' end, he dashed to the front door and threw it open, only to gasp in horror at the sight of two tall men clothed in dazzling white, standing right on his doorstep. In voices that were like rolling thunder the men spoke to him, saying, *"Why do you seek the living among the dead?"*

"Even while you were away," explained one, "the Lord Jesus Christ came back to earth, just as He promised. And now you have missed Him!"

Herbert George slammed the door shut in their faces, covered his ears, and sank to his knees. From that point on, he found that he literally could not get up again. His knees seemed to be locked tight. Even if he could have moved, he could not think straight about what to do. And yet he had to do something. With plaster raining all about his ears, he had to get away. In desperation, crawling agonizingly on hands and knees, he began inching his way down the hallway in the direction of the garage. As he passed the bathroom window, out of the corner of one eye he saw with a shiver that the sky was no longer red but bright black, black as obsidian, and pouring down bloody fire.

"The time machine ... the time machine ..." he whimpered. His machine was his only hope.

To his unimaginable dismay, however, as he reached the garage and managed to stumble through the doorway, he saw clearly that his beloved time machine was no longer there! In fact, not only was the cherished conveyance gone, but in its place, rising straight up through the roof for hundreds of stories into the ragged and tortured flesh of the heavens, was an enormous wooden cross, flashing like lightning and turning slowly back and forth like a flaming sword held in a warning hand, as though guarding the entrance to eternity.

* * *

Why do you long for the Day of the Lord?
  That day will be darkness, not light.
It will be as though a man fled from a lion,
  only to meet a bear;
as though he entered his house
  and put his hand on the wall,
  only to have a snake bite him.
    Amos 5:18-19

True North

ONCE THERE WERE FOUR GEESE who didn't always see eye to eye.

One day, at the first sign of spring, when the time had arrived for embarking upon their annual northern migration, it so happened that a great wind arose, blowing toward the south.

"Well, that settles it," blurted out one of the geese. "This year I'm flying south!"

"South!" honked the other fellows in alarm. "But that's crazy! You know we always fly north in the spring."

"You birds can do whatever you want," retorted the first goose. "But I aim to take advantage of this wind."

And with that, he lifted off into the breeze, and the other three watched as he disappeared over the southern horizon.

The very next day, as it turned out, the wind shifted slightly, so that now it was blowing toward the west.

"West!" honked the youngest goose gleefully. "Oh, West! I've always dreamed of flying west. So long, fellows!"

"But wait!" shouted the other two. "We're supposed to be going north!"

"North, schmorth!" cried the youngest goose, already airborne. "Just look at this beautiful wind!"

And off he went.

Just one day later, as fortune would have it, the wind shifted yet again, and this time it was a most dramatic change, from westerly all the way around to due east. And at that, without so much as a how-do-you-do, one of the two remaining geese stretched out his long neck and began his take-off.

"Hold on!" honked his partner. "Wait one more day and the wind may change!"

But it was no use. Already his friend was lost in the red swirl of the sunrise.

Sure enough, in the early hours of the fourth day, the wind did begin a gentle swing around to the north, until by mid-morning it had swelled into a good stiff breeze—enough to make the very heart of a goose soar. Here, indeed, was the very wind for which all four of them had originally been waiting. Yet now there was only one goose left to take advantage of it.

And so, all alone, one goose spread wide his great white wings, and all alone one goose felt his heavy body grow light as a single feather and rise up and up as he gave himself to the fresh, to the good, to the wonderful northerly wind.

But there was just one problem:

When it came to long distances, geese always flew in V-formation. Everybody knew that. One goose must fly in front, taking the full brunt of resistance in order that the others might travel more easily in the shadow of his wings. And all the strongest geese had to take their turn as leader, spelling each other off on the long and arduous journey.

Thus, flying together in formation, a flock of geese became a most beautiful and efficient thing: They became like one solitary pair of wings, like a single organism, like one strong and graceful bird.

But when geese could not get along, and when geese followed their own whims and went flying off in different directions, then they no longer behaved like a single integrated wing, nor did they become like one great and glorious bird. In fact, if the truth be told, geese who insisted on having their own way stopped being birds at all. They stopped having wings of their own, and instead became just so many feathers scattered to the four corners of the horizon.

And so it happened that even the goose who had waited patiently for the right wind, the good wind, and who flew north—True North—even he, alas! ...

The Furniture of Heaven & Other Parables for Pilgrims

NEVER MADE IT.

* ✲ *

A new commandment I give to you: that you love one another.
    John 13:34

www.ingramcontent.com/pod-product-compliance
Lightning Source LLC
Chambersburg PA
CBHW022109150426
43195CB00008B/331